THE REVOLUTIONS OF 1848

Studies in European History

General Editor: Richard Overy
Editorial Consultants: John Breuilly
                             Roy Porter

PUBLISHED TITLES

FORTHCOMING

Byun Kim

THE REVOLUTIONS OF 1848

ROGER PRICE

HUMANITIES PRESS INTERNATIONAL, INC.
Atlantic Highlands, NJ

First published in 1989 in the United States of America by
Humanities Press International, Inc.
Atlantic Highlands, NJ 07716

Reprinted 1990

Library of Congress Cataloging-in-Publication Data
Price, Roger.
The revolutions of 1848/Roger Price.
p.   cm.—(Studies in European history)
Bibliography: p.
Includes index.
ISBN 0–391–03595–9
1. Europe—History—1848–1849—Historiography.   I. Title.
II. Series.
D387.P75 1989
940.2'84'0072—dc19   88–13059
                                                      CIP

Printed in the United States of America

Contents

Acknowledgements

I would like to express my gratitude to the following good friends whose comments on earlier drafts of this essay contributed a great deal to the final version: my colleague Richard Evans, Colin Heywood of the University of Nottingham, Olena Heywood, and especially Heather Price. In addition I would like to thank the general editor of *Studies in European History*, Richard Overy, and his editorial consultants both for inviting me to write on 1848 and for their constructive suggestions. Vanessa Couchman and Vanessa Graham successively Humanities editors at Macmillan have consistently been supportive. Richard, Siân, Emily and Hannah also played their part – in many different ways!

RP

List of Maps

A Note on References

References are cited throughout in brackets according to the numbering in the select bibliography, with page references where necessary indicated by a colon after the bibliography number.

Editor's Preface

The main purpose of this new series of studies is to make available to teacher and student alike developments in a field of history that has become increasingly specialised with the sheer volume of new research and literature now produced. These studies are designed to present the 'state of the debate' on important themes and episodes in European history since the sixteenth century, presented in a clear and critical way by someone who is closely concerned himself with the debate in question.

The studies are not intended to be read as extended bibliographical essays, though each will contain a detailed guide to further reading which will lead students and the general reader quickly to key publications. Each book carries its own interpretation and conclusions, while locating the discussion firmly in the centre of the current issues as historians see them. It is intended that the series will introduce students to historical approaches which are in some cases very new and which, in the normal course of things, would take many years to filter down into the textbooks and school histories. I hope it will demonstrate some of the excitement historians, like scientists, feel as they work away in the vanguard of their subject.

The format of the series conforms closely with that of the companion volumes of studies in economic and social history which has already established a major reputation since its inception in 1968. Both series have an important contribution to make in publicising what it is that historians are doing and in making history more open and accessible. It is vital for history to communicate if it is to survive.

R. J. OVERY

Introduction

The year 1848 saw Europe convulsed by a wave of revolutions. Unprecedented in their scale and dimensions, they shook the political and social order to its foundations. The reaction which then followed, as established elites sought to restore their control through a combination of repression and limited measures of reform, was to be crucial to the development of social relationships in industrialising societies and to the evolution of the modern state.

The revolutions formed the culmination of a series of crises – economic, social and political – which occurred in the late 1840s. They began with poor harvests, and were deepened by an international financial and industrial crisis. The consequences were widespread hunger, disease, unemployment and business failure.

This short book will attempt to set a complicated, multi-faceted crisis within the longer term context of a continent already disturbed by the French Revolution and wars from 1789 to 1815 and the liberal and democratic aspirations established then. The pace of social change appeared to be accelerating, and with complex and uncertain results. In the middle years of the nineteenth century Europe was composed of regional and national societies undergoing transition from essentially pre-industrial economic and social structures towards more modern urban-industrial systems. The societies themselves varied, and so inevitably did the processes of change they experienced. In their diversity there lies an obvious analytical problem – that of taking into account differences in national geography and climate (at their most extreme ranging from the northern tundra to the Mediterranean); in levels of economic and social development (from Britain to Russia); in population densities; in structures of ownership and social relationships in agriculture (from

1

societies dominated by the large estate to those based upon small-scale peasant ownership) and in industry (from the factory to the workshop and the domestic producer); in settlement structures and patterns of internal relationships and of links with the external world (varying between the city and dispersed farms); in forms of culture and language; and in political systems (from constitutional monarchy to absolutism), and the opportunities for expressing grievances. All these factors are relevant to an examination of processes of politicisation and of political conflict. Against this background our primary concern will be with the causes of revolution; its subsequent course; and the reasons for the rapid development and success of counter-revolution. In addition to the analysis of revolution, explanations will be offered as to why, in this 'Year of Revolutions', much of Europe remained comparatively peaceful.

Both contemporaries and historians have inevitably sought to explain events of such magnitude. Their approaches have been inspired by their own practical concerns and political outlook. Conservative, liberal, radical and socialist analyses can be identified[110], although more dispassionate approaches have developed as the events themselves have become more distant. The evolution of the discipline of history, particularly from the 1960s, has stimulated also a renewal of the study of revolution. A broadening of the historians' range of enquiry has occurred, going beyond the traditional concern with political behaviour narrowly defined, to examine the social roots of politics, and develop detailed local and regional studies in order to engage in the analysis of social relationships, the structure of power, its symbolism and language[30]. The creative adaptation of research techniques and conceptual frameworks developed initially by sociologists, anthropologists and other social scientists has allowed historians to take greater advantage of the mass of information thrown up by the events of 1848, and to offer to the social sciences in return a better understanding of social systems undergoing processes of modernisation both in the past and the present.

Concerned as we are to make sense of a series of events affecting an entire continent, the selection of key questions is obviously of crucial significance. Something, therefore, needs

2

to be said about the criteria for selection, as well as to justify the broadly comparative approach which will be adopted. What is an acceptable level of generalisation? The danger in writing a book organised around concepts and themes is that the uniqueness of particular revolutions, and even more of events at a local level, will be lost. The comparative approach does offer certain advantages, however. It stimulates analysis. Moreover, in 1848 Europeans did share to some extent in a sense of 'general malaise'[15]. Furthermore, as they developed, the various revolutionary movements were to some degree interdependent, and each passed through similar stages, lending support to the notion that 'the factors leading to the uprising transcended state boundaries'[99], and perhaps confirming that social groups reacted in similar fashion throughout Europe. These stages will supply the basic organis-ational structure for this book.

It is not my intention to suggest that there is a simple model or theory which will provide a ready-made explanation of the events of 1848. Political unrest occurred in extremely diverse societies. With the exception of Britain and Belgium, pre-industrial economic and social structures remained to a large degree intact, reinforced by poor communications and geographical isolation. In most of Central and Eastern Europe the institutions of serfdom and of absolutism were still very much alive. Germany and Italy were both made up of a number of competing sovereign states. The Habsburg Empire, with its twenty kingdoms, archduchies, duchies, counties, etc., most with their own 'estates', was also characterised by major internal economic, social and linguistic differences. To a lesser extent the same was true everywhere. Inevitably such differences in economic structures, in social organisation, in patterns of communication and in political institutions affected the forms of political consciousness and activity. It is thus essential to seek an understanding of the social contexts for political behaviour, and at the same time to remind ourselves that there are no safe and easy generalisations to be made about the links between the levels of economic development and political relationships.

3

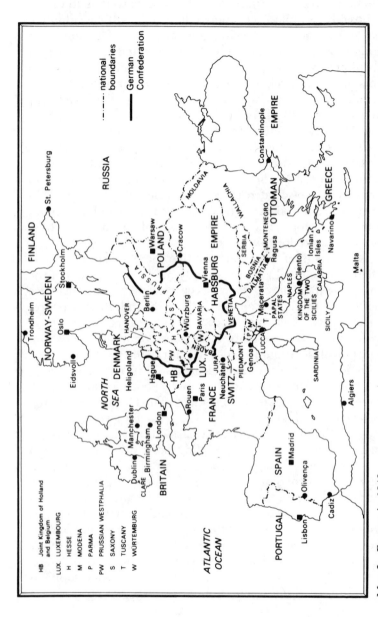

Map I Europe in 1848.
Source: C. Church, *Europe in 1830* (Allen & Unwin, 1983), p. 181. (This map was originally entitled: Europe, about 1835. There were no major boundary changes before 1848)

4

1 Social Systems

Far too often historians, obsessed with the drama of politics, have taken 1789 to be *the* turning point in modern European history. They would appear to have had good reason. The assault upon monarchy, the nobility and church in France, the destructive consequences of interminable war, and the determination of the allies in 1815 to ensure that revolution would never again threaten the established social and political order, had prolonged effects. Nevertheless it needs to be stressed that economic structures and social systems – even in France – changed only slowly. The populations of Europe in the 1840s remained predominantly rural. Industrial workers made up 25 per cent or more of the population only in Britain, France and Belgium and most of these worked in small workshops. Even in Britain less than 10 per cent of the population was employed in factories. Poor communications and fragmented markets, together with low incomes and purchasing power restricted the development of large-scale, homogeneous markets. For the same reasons, industry remained largely dependent upon local sources of raw materials – using water wheels rather than steam engines as power sources, and wood rather than coal as fuel. Production was frequently dispersed through the countryside to take advantage of underemployed and low-cost rural labour and was closely integrated into rural society.

However, change was clearly evident, and its pace accelerating. Towns played a crucial role in this process, serving as the commercial centres from which merchants organised the 'putting-out' of raw materials and orders for manufactures into rural hinterlands where overpopulation and seasonal underemployment provided reserves of cheap labour. In recent years this development has been seen as a distinct 'proto-industrial' phase in European economic history. At the same time the central position of some towns in existing communications networks, and the access this provided to supplies of raw materials and extensive markets encouraged the development of larger-scale factory production. More characteristic was the complex of small enterprises producing all manner of goods, from luxuries for the wealthy, to such necessities as clothing and bread, engaged in building, and the provision of a wide variety of services. While the numerous workshops offered employment to highly skilled and relatively well-rewarded artisans, the cities also offered shelter to a mass of unskilled workers – street-traders, porters, dockers, general labourers – living from hand to mouth, in a state of permanent insecurity. Marx borrowed the Neapolitan term *lazzaroni* to describe this class, as well as coining his own label – lumpenproletariat.

With the exception of a small number of rapidly growing industrial centres, the majority of towns remained pre-industrial in structure and medieval in appearance. This was true even of the capital cities of Europe, of the primary centres of revolution in 1848. Rapid population growth burdened them with accumulations of desperately poor people, crowded together in squalid warrens. Even outside the city centres, in developing suburbs where space existed for new factories, new slums were created as workers able to afford only minimal rents crowded into hastily constructed housing.

In spite of these important elements of continuity the factory was the symbol of a new age. Together with mechanised production, it had developed first in Britain for a complex of reasons, and especially the gradual development from at least the seventeenth century of relatively large, integrated markets due to comparatively easy access to most of the island allowed by inland waterways and the sea, to relatively high per capita incomes, and the availability of natural resources. Other Europeans regarded Britain with a mixture of horror and fascination. They frequently condemned the working and living conditions imposed on the industrial labour force, partly from fear that this might lead to revolt. Nevertheless the new techniques were increasingly adopted. This appeared to be the only means of avoiding the destructive consequences

6

of British competition and might offer profitable business opportunities.

The impact of the growth of mechanised production upon existing artisanal manufacture was both direct – as machines began to replace hand-work especially in the textile trades, provoking on occasion machine-breaking and riots, as in Silesia in 1844 – and indirect, when the wholesale merchants who controlled the supply of raw materials and access to the markets for the finished products produced in artisanal workshops, as well as the crucial credit facilities, increasingly put pressure upon their suppliers to reduce their costs. The effect of this was to impose a reorganisation of work processes, and most clearly to reinforce the divisions of labour within craft workshops. These trends threatened not only to reduce the incomes of skilled workers, but also to degrade their 'art'. It threatened the quality of their lives, and made it increasingly less likely that the more ambitious would ever become master-artisans with their own workshops. Inevitably these developments caused increased tensions in the workplace and between master-artisans and merchants.

Economic change was a threat not only to the viability of particular trades, but also to the prosperity of entire regions. Map II provides an impression of the spatial characteristics of economic change. Clearly not all areas in which manufacture expanded in the eighteenth and early nineteenth centuries possessed the capital and natural resources necessary for modern industrial development. As development occurred some regions, and rural areas in general, experienced de-industrialisation. The centres of early industrialisation – in textiles, mining, metallurgy and engineering – were islands in the midst of a rural sea.

In certain other crucial respects the *ancien régime* could also be said to have survived well into the nineteenth century. Even where, as in France, constitutional monarchy had been established, the monarch retained the substantial authority believed by elites to be essential to the preservation of order. Further east, absolute monarchy survived with little more than the force of custom, local privilege, and practical realities (small bureaucracies, limited incomes, poor communications,

7

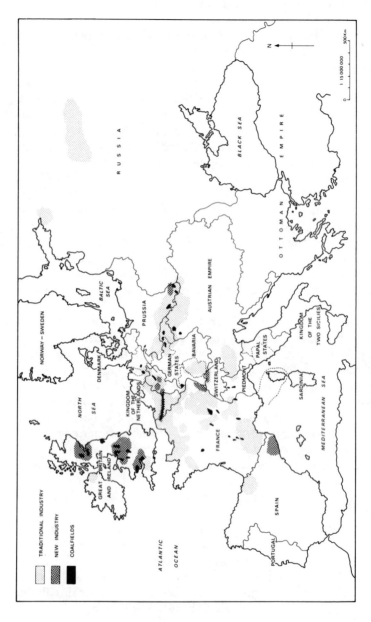

Map II   Industrial development. Europe in 1815 (above) compared with Europe in 1875 (below).
Source: S. Pollard, *Peaceful Conquest* (Oxford University Press, 1981)

8

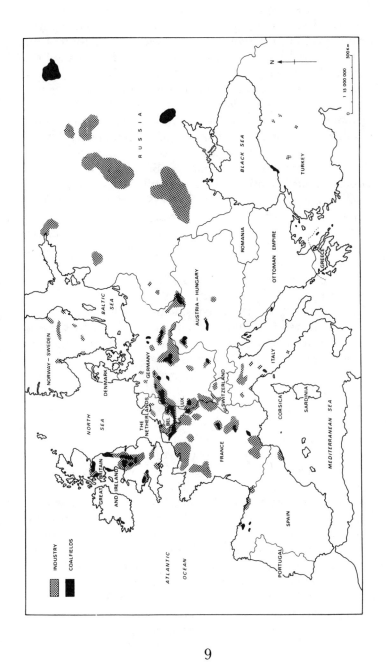

INDUSTRY

COALFIELDS

NORWAY – SWEDEN

RUSSIA

BALTIC SEA

DENMARK

NORTH SEA

GREAT BRITAIN AND IRELAND

THE NETHERLANDS

GERMANY

BEL.

LUX.

SWITZERLAND

AUSTRIA – HUNGARY

ROMANIA

BLACK SEA

OTTOMAN EMPIRE

TURKEY

GREECE

ATLANTIC OCEAN

FRANCE

CORSICA

SARDINIA

ITALY

MEDITERRANEAN SEA

PORTUGAL

SPAIN

N

1 : 15 000 000

0   500 km.

9

etc.) to enforce restraint. Furthermore, aristocratic landowners retained positions of social and political predominance, even in Britain and France, where wealth, and the adoption of the appropriate life-style, had allowed successful members of the professional and business classes to accede to positions of influence. The further east one looked the more complete was aristocratic dominance, protected as it was by the institutions of absolute monarchy. In predominantly rural societies, those with a disproportionate share in the possession of wealth were able to control access to scarce resources (and particularly the land), to employment, and to charity. Because of their virtual monopoly of key positions in representative assemblies, the bureaucracy and the army, they dominated the process of law-making and controlled the means of coercion and so possessed multi-faceted means of exercising power. In western Europe, as Map III suggests, landlord power was based upon the tenanted farm; in central and eastern Europe it was reinforced by the survival of feudal relationships. Even where peasant proprietorship predominated, a minority of larger landowners usually exercised considerable influence.

Semi-feudal tenures and serfdom prevailed, with varying degrees of severity, in eastern Germany, most of the Habsburg Empire, Russia, and the Danubian principalities of Moldavia and Wallachia. In Prussia, liberation of the serfs had occurred on terms which, while they had allowed the emergence of a minority of prosperous peasants, had left most of the rural population with little or no land. This gave them no choice but to work as labourers for landowners who retained control of the local administration and police, who paid hardly any taxes themselves, and who might, if they felt so inclined, provide minimal assistance to 'their' peasants in times of need. Elsewhere in the east most peasants held only usufructuary rights over the land, that is rights of usage in return for obligatory labour services (usually 3–4 days a week, longer at harvests), and other dues, which theoretically compensated their landlords for the exercise of those judicial and police functions which in reality substantially increased their power[2]. While frequently aware of the inefficiencies of a system in which peasants sought to conserve their energy when working the lord's land, for work on their own plots,

Map III Predominant types of land tenure in Europe in 1848.
Source: Open University, *The Revolutions of 1848* (Unit 2, Milton Keynes, 1976)

landlords were afraid that change might threaten the stability of the entire social system.

With the exception of southern England, parts of northern France, of the Low Countries and north-eastern Germany where intensive, commercially-orientated mixed farming had developed, farming practices remained backward and yields low and susceptible to unfavourable climatic conditions. The continuous growth of population in a period when industry and commerce were unable to create sufficient additional employment opportunities meant growing numbers of people competing for a limited number of places as agricultural

11

labourers, or in rural industry, or to rent and purchase farms. It reinforced the power of those who controlled scarce resources, permitting them to force wages down and rents and land prices up. The poor were obliged to accept conditions of dependence, and to tolerate relationships into which the wealthy normally assumed they had freely entered. Moreover the traditional paternalistic ethos which had at least offered some protection against the worst extremes of misery was breaking down. The gradual improvement of communications, the development of commercial agriculture and the monetisation of economic relationships encouraged landowners, large farmers and the better-off peasants to exploit the land more efficiently by such means as enclosure and restrictions upon the traditional rights of access to forests for fuel and pasture upon which poor peasants often depended.

Although contemporary social commentators tended to focus upon the new social problems represented by industrial growth and urban overcrowding, the difficulties caused by rural overpopulation should not be underestimated. In spite of increasing agricultural productivity, much of the rural population lived in poverty even in good years, and this degenerated into misery and even starvation when harvests were poor (Map IV).

In such circumstances rural unrest was normal and the 1840s saw major agrarian riots in East Prussia, Silesia and Posen, and most alarmingly of all a *jacquerie* in Galicia in February and March 1846 when hundreds of Polish noble families were slaughtered. In general, however, the expression of grievances was restrained by fear of the repressive consequences. Moreover, the social hierarchy was justified by a complex of secular and religious ideologies which together produced a diffuse but socially conservative culture. As an 1803 Prussian decree on education typically stipulated, 'the children of the working class are to be taught to read the Catechism, Bible and Hymn Book; to fear and love God and act accordingly; to honour authority'. In effect the superior capacity for organisation and exercising influence possessed by relatively coherent elites meant that the use of force to preserve their position was not normally necessary, although the threat was always present[101].

12

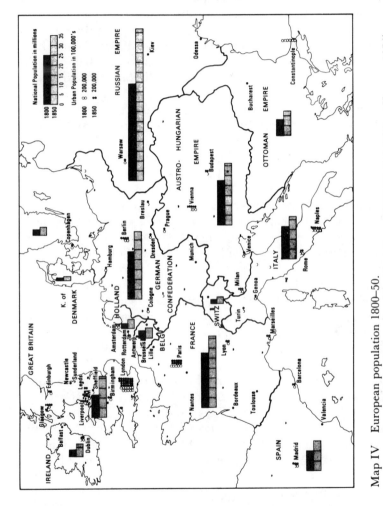

Map IV European population 1800–50.
Source: Open University, *The Revolutions of 1848* (Unit 2, Milton Keynes, 1976)

13

This was certainly the case in the decades after 1815. Concern that revolutionary outbreaks might recur seemed justified by the events of 1830. Then, in France economic crisis and widespread social unrest combined with Charles X's unwillingness to contemplate liberal reforms, and his decision to resort to political repression had stimulated protest which led to clashes between demonstrators and the forces of order in Paris, to governmental collapse and revolution. These events had encouraged protest elsewhere – most notably in the southern Netherlands where discontent, especially amongst the middle classes about tax and tariff structures which appeared to favour the Dutch, and the government's educational and linguistic policies, led to revolt and – with French support – the establishment of a separate Belgian kingdom. Widespread disorders also occurred in southern Germany, central Italy and in Poland, where a revolt took place against Russian rule. The result in this last case was brutal repression. Elsewhere, and especially in France, Britain, Belgium, the Netherlands and the states of southern Germany, concessions were made to liberal demands. These had the effect of enfranchising mainly relatively well-off sections of the middle classes and on the Continent of reinforcing parliamentary powers. They represented efforts by governments to reinforce social stability by means of the integration of property owners (generally defined as those paying a minimum amount in direct taxation) into the political system. Most people continued to be excluded because they were female or because they possessed neither the material stake in society nor the education which it was assumed were necessary to allow them to take a responsible, an informed, and a rational part in political decision-making. This fundamental inequality was reinforced by discriminatory taxation, and (on the Continent) by military conscription from which the better-off tended to be exempt; and by continuing restrictions on civil liberties. In the aftermath of 1830 the Papal encyclical *Mirari Vos* published in August 1832 represented widely held conservative views in describing liberty of the press as 'the deadly freedom' and warned that: 'States have perished from this single evil, unrestrained freedom of thought, freedom of speech and the love of novelties'[9, 109].

In spite of such restrictions, reform represented recognition of changes in social structures and values. Commercialisation, urbanisation, the development of bureaucracy, and the extension of manufacture combined to increase the numbers and pretensions of the urban middle classes. Yet nowhere had the transition to a modern economy advanced sufficiently to bring about the substantial improvement in the conditions of the masses which might have alleviated their discontent. Population pressure on the resources of agriculture, the decline of rural industry and the intensely competitive character of early industrialisation combined to create widespread misery and a growing fear of social unrest within the possessing classes. This was the environment within which the 1848 Revolutions occurred.

2 The Background Causes of Revolution in 1848

An examination of the causes of revolution involves its own particular problems. The relevant factors include socio-economic structures; the impact of shorter term economic circumstances; the existence of political opposition, and the capacity of governments to deal with it. Revolution – or indeed its absence – can only be understood within the context of particular social and political systems. Moreover, although the classification of causal variables is a necessary analytical tool, the distinctions made are all, to some degree, arbitrary and artificial. Weighting the significance of each is extremely difficult and the efforts of political scientists to develop explanatory theories have led, all too often, to tautology and oversimplification. It might help, to begin with, to distinguish between the background factors – the preconditions – and the actual precipitants of revolutionary action. In this it is important to remember that very few people actually wanted or expected revolution. Indeed, for the vast majority of politically active people the memory and myths of 1789 served as a great deterrent to overstepping the bounds of 'normal' political activity. In order to understand why established authority collapsed in so many places we have to try to manage without the benefits of hindsight, and seek comprehension of the psychology and behaviour of the historical actors by making an imaginative leap into the past. Revolution has to be considered as both a political event and a social process.

The decisive factor in 1848 was the coincidence between severe economic and social crisis and political difficulties. Pre-existing social tensions were intensified by the crisis. Policy disagreements within elites and demands for liberalisation took on greater urgency as doubt was thrown upon the legitimacy of existing institutions by the patent inability of governments to cope with such pressing problems as the relief of poverty and the maintenance of law and order, and by their continuing unwillingness to make concessions in such matters as censorship, the electoral franchise and the powers of representative assemblies. This was a situation promoting mobilisation. For this to turn into revolution, 'triggering' incidents were necessary although once one government had fallen, the widespread lack of confidence already evident within governing circles was likely to take its toll.

It is clear that the development, from 1845, of a severe economic crisis greatly intensified the social problems caused by population growth and industrialisation. In most respects this crisis was typical of those of the *ancien régime économique* described by Ernest Labrousse[14]. The impact of poor cereal harvests in 1845 and 1846 together with potato blight was magnified by slow and expensive communications, the inefficient diffusion of information, the difficulties experienced in balancing regional and international supplies, and by panic buying on the part of consumers and speculation by merchants[60]. A substantial rise in food prices occurred over most of Europe – frequently by over 50 per cent in particular localities, with complex effects on commercial, financial and industrial activity, already suffering from a cyclical downswing.

One obvious effect of rising food prices was to threaten the already low living standards of the mass of poor people in town and country. Furthermore, expenditure on manufactured goods declined as larger proportions of their incomes were spent on foodstuffs, with the result that at the very moment that the prices of basic necessities rose, so too did unemployment in both urban and rural industry. The crisis was further deepened by the deflationary effects of an outflow of bullion to finance food imports, of rising interest rates, and by the repatriation of British capital, which had, in more prosperous times, been invested in Continental railways and industrial development[47, 75, 77]. This contraction of credit caused liquidity crises for many businessmen, led to numerous bankruptcies and added to the general air of insecurity. In a transition economy the impact of a pre-industrial subsistence crisis was made all the more severe by the development of the overproduction/underconsumption crisis more typical of an industrial economy.

The social and geographical impact of the crisis inevitably varied. In the British Isles cereal harvests were mediocre in 1845, but not particularly bad in 1846. Moreover, with its relatively advanced economy, involvement in overseas commerce, and regular dependence on food imports, Britain was well placed to secure additional supplies. This renders the experience of Ireland, which suffered the full impact of potato blight, and where over half a million people died of starvation or famine-related diseases, all the more inexcusable. Peel's relief measures, themselves in no way adequate to the scale of the crisis, were subsequently cut back by the Whigs, inspired by a combination of liberal economic theory, with its stress on the efficient workings of the free market in foodstuffs, and the view that government intervention would only lead to budgetary deficit and, worse still, encourage the 'natural' improvidence of the Irish population. There was a generalised lack of understanding of the problems of Ireland and indeed, outside official circles preoccupied by the threat of disorder in Ireland and amongst Irish migrants to the mainland, little interest in events which had only limited direct impact upon the British themselves. Even mainland Britain suffered, however, from increased unemployment. A survey of 179 factories in Manchester in March 1847 revealed that of a normal workforce of 40,000, 19,000 were on short-time or out of work. Nevertheless with the exception of textiles, and partly due to the counter-cyclical impact of railway construction, the crisis does not appear to have been exceptionally severe – in terms of its effects on employment and wages less so than that of 1840–2. The depression subsequently caused by the 1848 Revolutions would have a far more serious impact[157]. In the east too, in Russia and parts of Poland, grain crops were reasonably good. Conditions seem to have been at their worst in Ireland, in Belgian Flanders, Prussian Silesia and Austrian Galicia.

If everywhere it was the unskilled and propertyless who suffered most, the intensity of their misery varied according to a complex of factors including, obviously, local population densities and agricultural productivity, together with the

19

capacity of merchants to respond to local shortages, the structure of landownership and nature of employment opportunities and the willingness and ability of local officials and elites to undertake relief measures[58, 59]. Humanitarianism, together with the desire to prevent disorder, encouraged the latter. It was rarely on a scale sufficient to prevent the rise of social tension, manifesting itself through strikes, demonstrations, increased criminality and food riots[60, 75, 92, 127] such as the so-called 'potato revolt' – three days of rioting and attacks on food shops in Berlin in April 1847. Although not in itself likely to lead to revolution, a crisis of this kind generated a widespread sense of grievance amongst those who felt that it was the duty of governments to take some form of positive action. These included the hungry and unemployed, businessmen threatened with bankruptcy, peasants anxious about foreclosure for debt, and all those frightened by unrest and disorder. The sense of malaise was expressed by Count Galen, Prussian representative at Kassel, writing on 20 January 1847: 'The old year ended in scarcity, the new one opens with starvation. Misery, spiritual and physical, traverses Europe in ghastly shapes – the one without God, the other without bread. Woe if they join hands!' Although conditions tended to improve from the autumn of 1847, after a good harvest, unemployment remained high, indebtedness widespread and insecurity intense. The real danger, from the point of view of government, was the politicisation of this discontent. This occurred for a variety of reasons[28].

In itself, misery did not lead directly or inevitably to political mobilisation. Indeed, where conditions were at their worst, as in Ireland, the starving had more pressing concerns – although in the longer term hatred of British rule was massively reinforced. In economically more advanced societies, although the social difficulties caused by urbanisation and industrialisation were not irrelevant to the rise of discontent, this only became dangerous to established governments, when it received a political focus. Even then the possible courses of action varied according to differences in political culture and institutions and with perceptions of the opportunities for expressing grievances. The decisive factor appears to have been the aggravation of discontent within middle-class groups

20

possessing the organisational capacity which facilitated the mobilisation both of wider circles of the *bourgeoisie* and of mass support. In ideological terms their demands were expressed largely through liberalism, a creed which varied considerably according to local social and political circumstances, and which frequently represented a desire for 'modernisation' on the British model. Their objectives included the end of arbitrary government through a reduction in the power of such traditional institutions as the monarchy and church, a wider sharing of political power by means of the development of parliamentary government, together with guarantees of individual freedoms and the rule of law. Liberals generally rejected democracy and the sovereignty of the people which were thought likely to produce anarchy, in favour of rule by those with the real, that is propertied, stake in society, which it was assumed would guarantee rational and responsible behaviour. They most certainly were not advocates of political change by means of revolution[46, 101, 119, 122].

The reforms requested, and the tactics employed, varied according to the situations in which political activists found themselves. Inevitably there were also substantial differences of emphasis and objectives amongst opposition politicians. In Britain, Belgium and France the upper and part of the middle, middle class had already been enfranchised although traditional elites retained a prominent role in government. Only in France would revolution occur. Further east noble dominance was more blatant – in Prussia in 1842 nobles held 9 of 11 ministries and 20 of 28 provincial governorships[9]. Growing numbers of professional men – civil servants, lawyers, doctors, journalists – and businessmen felt undervalued and resented what they saw as the failure of successive governments to give sufficient consideration to their vital interests. Between these educated and propertied representatives of the *bourgeoisie* and the mass of workers and peasants, a lower middle class made up especially of shopkeepers and master-artisans served as a bridge, frequently sharing the political concerns of those above them in the social hierarchy, but also much of the insecurity of the poor.

Poverty as a social problem had attracted considerable interest in the 1840s, evidence of a deepening sense of social

21

crisis. This could be found on the one hand in numerous official and private enquiries, and on the other in the humanitarian socialism of the Frenchmen Blanc, Cabet, Leroux and Proudhon or the German Weitling, whose slogans, including the 'emancipation of the working class' and 'the organisation of work', were taken up and discussed amongst the minority of skilled and literate workers, particularly those in the towns, already organised within guild structures in Central Europe and benefiting in France from surviving pre-revolutionary traditions of association. Many of them looked forward to the day when, through the formation of producers' cooperatives, they might become masters of their own destinies in a more egalitarian and harmonious society. The bases of this artisanal discontent were thus the traditional solidarities of the existing craft communities. Less skilled workers – employed in factories or as general labourers – often, in this transitional phase of industrial development, recent migrants into urban centres, generally lacked such a strong sense of commitment. Materially and culturally impoverished, they showed little interest in democratic or socialist ideas. Only in Britain, with its longer established working-class communities, was a wider but still limited cross-section of workers attracted to Chartism as a means of expressing their discontent with unregulated competition, low wages and poor working conditions, the threat of the workhouse for the impoverished and the all-pervading sense of political powerlessness[45, 61, 88, 164].

Where governments appeared unresponsive to these various grievances, in a situation of intense crisis like 1846–7, it is hardly surprising that protest and resistance to government policy should become more common, and that the circle of those normally interested in politics should be considerably widened. In France a variety of opposition groups including supporters of the regime, disappointed by the results of the 1846 elections and by their continued exclusion from office and patronage, together with more principled members of the republican opposition, pressed for an extension of the right to vote (beyond those paying 200 francs in direct taxes) that is, they sought to change the rules of the political game as the only means by which they might gain power. They combined in July 1847 to initiate a campaign in favour of reform and managed to circumvent the laws against political meetings by presenting these as convivial banquets. The government's continuing intransigence served only to radicalise this movement, with radical republicans, most notably Ledru-Rollin, who favoured manhood suffrage, assuming an increasingly prominent role at the expense of members of the dynastic opposition such as Odilon Barrot. The campaign was planned to culminate in a mass banquet in Paris on 22 February 1848, and it was official efforts to prevent this gathering which led directly to revolution[55, 71]. In Prussia the accession of Friedrich Wilhelm IV in 1840 had been followed by a relaxation of censorship, and the creation of a commission made up of representatives of the provincial diets which would meet in Berlin once every two years in order to offer advice to the monarch. These moves had encouraged liberals, especially in the economically relatively advanced Rhineland – through such spokesmen as Hansemann, Camphausen and Mevissen – to press for a constitutional regime. A situation in which the 100,000 inhabitants of Cologne and Aachen were represented in the Rhenish diet by 3 delegates, while the 7000 nobles had 25 representatives, and the fact that throughout the Prussian state there were twice as many noble as *bourgeois* members of diets was becoming increasingly unacceptable. Wealthy non-nobles were anxious to secure more effective representation of their interests in matters of taxation and customs duties, and to reduce bureaucratic interference in their affairs. Professional men, finding it difficult to obtain the posts for which their university education seemed to qualify them, complained about the preference shown to nobles. More generally the arbitrariness and petty tyranny exercised by state officials was increasingly resented, and the desire expressed for the reinforcement of the rule of law, and the establishment of a *Rechtsstaat* (i.e a state based upon the rule of law). In such matters as censorship, where the regulations were frequently circumvented both by clandestine publishing and the smuggling of illicit materials, and by the use of 'aesopian' language – complex allusions and political criticism disguised as literary or social commentary – repression was sufficient to cause considerable discontent, but incapable of stemming the growing tide of protest[122].

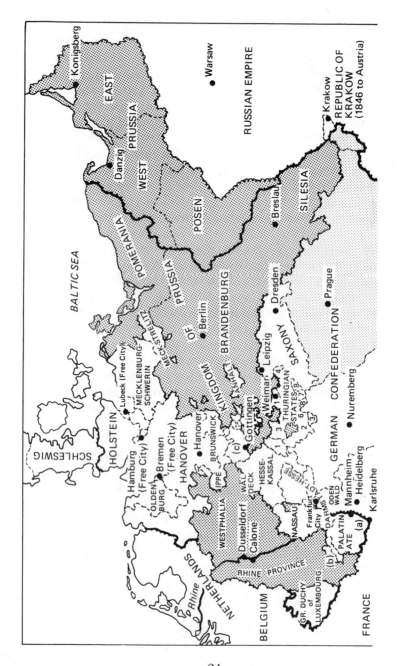

24

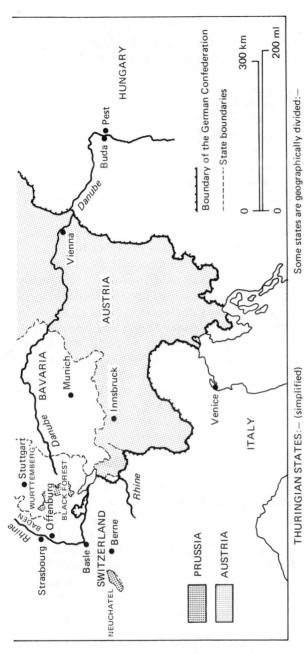

THURINGIAN STATES:— (simplified)

1 Saxe-Weimar	5 Schwarzburg-Sondershausen
2 Saxe-Meiningen	6 Schwarzburg-Rudolstaadt
3 Saxe-Coburg-Gotha	7 Reuss-Schleiz
4 Saxe-Altenburg	8 Reuss-Greiz

Some states are geographically divided:—

Bavaria and (a) Palatinate

Oldenburg and (b)

Hanover and (c)

Boundary of the German Confederation

------ State boundaries

PRUSSIA

AUSTRIA

Map V   Germany in 1848.
Source: H. Holborn, *A History of Modern Germany* (Eyre & Spottiswoode, 1965)

Influenced to a large degree by the 'disruption of traditional loyalties during the revolutionary era'[119] the desire for liberalisation was particularly intense in Baden, the Bavarian Palatinate, parts of Württemberg and Hanover and the western provinces of Prussia – particularly the Rhineland. Here the desire to defend provincial institutions, including the *Code civil* inherited from the period of French rule, and the interests of the Roman Catholic church, together with resentment of the centralist Prussian bureaucracy on the part of an increasingly self-confident *bourgeoisie* combined to stimulate demands for a constitutional monarchy, and the enfranchisement of the wealthy, on the model of the French constitution of 1830. The leaders of this liberal movement, such as Camphausen and Mevissen in Cologne, were also aware, however, of the political advantages of the Prussian connection and of the economic benefits derived from membership of the Zollverein customs union. Thus all they really wanted was modest constitutional change together with some further progress towards greater German unity[122].

In the development of opposition politics in Germany much depended upon the local social and political climate. Subsequently regionalism and localism would substantially weaken the liberal and democratic movements. However, during 1846 and 1847 interest in politics was clearly growing, as could be seen from the formation of a variety of social clubs and professional associations which provided both a front for debate and a training in political organisation. These enabled many civil servants, lawyers, university professors and journalists, together with a not inconsiderable number of businessmen – men whose functions gave them a certain status, and who enjoyed the leisure which came with wealth, and the training in public speaking which was part of a classical education – to establish reputations for themselves. They conceived of their activities as representative of the spirit of reason, of the forces of the future in conflict with selfish vested interest. They were certain that history was on their side. Gradually their ideas spread down the social hierarchy, to be adopted, and adapted, by the lower middle classes and skilled workers[104].

Largely by this means a minority of journeymen artisans

most of whom belonged to the traditional guilds, or the more modern mutual aid societies and workers' educational associations (*Arbeiterbildungsvereine*), became aware of a complex of liberal, radical and even socialist ideas. However, in the prevailing pre-industrial situation most assumed that their interests would best be served by the protection of existing manufacture against industrial competition, by means of a reinforcement of guild privileges[88, 112].

That the adherents of this diffuse movement of 'liberal' political opposition so typical of the *Vormärz* period (i.e. the period from 1815 to 'pre-March' 1848) were far from agreeing on basic principles was evident from their attitudes towards the 'social problem'. These varied between a determination to blame the 'feckless' poor for their own misery, which could only be eased by rapid economic modernisation together with moral education to prevent the breakdown in the social order already evident in the growth of 'sexual licence', drunkenness, crime and socialism and a more compassionate desire to protect the interests of the small independent artisan and farmer against unrestrained capitalism. A minority of radicals – mainly intellectuals – were even prepared to support such measures as compulsory education and a progressive income tax. However, it was already evident, even before 1848, that popular unrest was leading many liberals to question their faith in progress, and to look to the state as a source of protection. Marx noted this ambivalence in pointing out that rich liberal merchants such as Hansemann and Camphausen were terrified of helping to establish a situation in which 'the rabble gets insolent and lays hands on things'[88].

Within Prussia the king's convocation of a United Diet in 1847 was a concession to these complex pressures, as well as being the intended but unsuccessful means of raising a loan. Although it was meant to serve only as a consultative assembly it provided a forum for the expression of grievances and the articulation of an idea of the constitutional state. As a result it was soon dissolved by the king. With his aristocratic advisers, he held to the conception of a Christian, Germanic monarchy whose authority was limited only by respect for the law and the liberties and privileges of the traditional orders and corporations. They appealed to tradition, the legitimacy of the established order, and issued warnings about the danger of another 1789. However, the fact of the Diet's meeting and the nature of its going only increased discontent[89, 95].

Similar unrest existed within the Austrian Empire. Influential works such as that published anonymously by a government official, Baron Andrian-Warburg, on *Austria and its Future* (1842), or articles published in the *Grenzboten*, a newspaper printed in Leipzig and smuggled across the frontier, attacked the inefficient bureaucracy, censorship, the taxation system, the centralisation of decision-making and the favouritism shown towards nobles. They stimulated the discussion of reform in such meeting places in Vienna as the Legal-Political Reading Club, which attracted officials and professional men, the Concordia Society, a forum for writers, artists and musicians, and the Lower Austrian Manufacturers' Association. By 1847 these bodies were holding joint sessions to discuss constitutional change. The Estates of Lower Austria, which because of the development of Vienna as an administrative, financial, commercial and manufacturing centre included increasingly assertive bourgeois elements, additionally pressed for the abolition of the last remaining feudal obligations, and for measures to relieve poverty. At the same time many nobles expressed resentment at their own exclusion from decision-making processes by a narrowly conservative court aristocracy[89, 143]. A further complication was the combination in Bohemia and Hungary of these diverse currents of opposition with nationalist discontent. In part, and especially in Hungary, this was encouraged by nobles appealing to historical provincial rights as a means of re-establishing their own political authority, but it also represented a widespread resentment of the increasingly Germanic character of the empire. Nationalistic sentiment had grown, particularly from the late eighteenth century, initially amongst intellectuals and students then increasingly as a more widespread movement of reaction against political domination, claims to social, cultural and linguistic superiority and economic competition. In the case of Germans the threat of French domination at the turn of the century had played a part in stimulating a national consciousness. But in Bohemia, Hungary and Northern Italy it was the German speakers who were identified as seeking hegemony although the Magyars were themselves also committed to efforts to secure their control over a variety of linguistically distinctive groups including Slovaks, Croats and Romanians (Map VI). The complex intermingling of ethnic groups, which had developed over many centuries, was to be of major political significance in 1848[3]. In Bohemia, where the nobles and *haute bourgeoisie* were essentially German-speaking or assimilated, a gradual process of widening and deepening of nationalist sentiment had occurred with new ideas spreading from the intellectual and professional classes to the small merchants and craftsmen in the towns, and better-off peasants in the more accessible and commercially active rural areas – the process of diffusion illustrating the importance of communications and cultural contact[142]. Nineteenth-century nationalist historians, however, exaggerated the strength of these feelings. Before 1848 only a small minority were actively interested in transforming the political situation of their ethnic group, and their influence was limited by censorship, lack of contact with the masses, and their own fear of arousing anarchical passions. Even so, these minorities, given their social roles, were potentially influential.

Increasingly, and particularly within the German and Italian states, national unity was claimed to be a prerequisite for political and economic modernisation. This combination of liberalism and nationalism was most clearly evident in Germany where the Confederation created in 1815, with its Diet meeting in Frankfurt, gave it limited institutional meaning, while at the same time reaffirming the independence of the 39 separate states[122]. In Italy localism appears to have had even firmer roots, in spite of the Austrian occupation of Lombardy and Venetia. Mazzini was one of the very few proponents of an unitary republic, and of revolutionary violence. Otherwise, in those areas directly controlled or else dominated by Austria, local elites made up of noble and non-noble landowners and the urban aristocracy of cities like Milan, together with wealthy professionals and merchants, felt unfairly excluded from government by foreigners. Furthermore the educated resented a censorship which banned Dante, Boccaccio, Hugo and Goethe from the universities; and businessmen objected to economic policies designed to favour

29

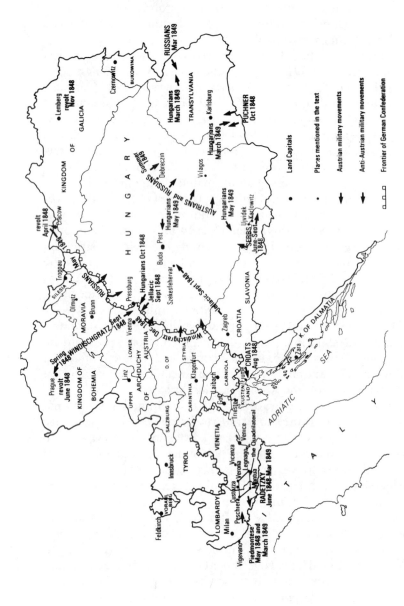

Map VI Habsburg Empire 1848-51.
Source: Open University, *The Revolutions of 1848* (Unit 2, Milton Keynes, 1976)

Austrian and Bohemian manufacturers. Even the clergy – especially influential in the countryside – objected to Austrian interference in ecclesiastical affairs. The role of these groups in the growth of opposition was to be crucial.

Nevertheless the failure of the insurrectionary movements of the 1820s had encouraged support for the more moderate approach espoused by men such as Cavour who favoured economic and political modernisation on British or French lines. It was the election of Pope Pius IX in June 1846, followed by an amnesty for 2000 political prisoners and relaxation of the censorship which provided the vital stimulus to liberal and nationalist sentiment throughout the peninsula. The governments of Tuscany and Piedmont felt obliged to make similar concessions and support grew for the idea of a confederation of Italian states presided over by the Pope. These developments alarmed conservatives, and indeed the pace of change and the emergence of more radical and democratic political groups, together with the prospect of war with Austria, frightened many moderates. Even so, in Lombardy-Venetia, the central and provincial assemblies (*congregations*) decided to support a proposal made by the democrats Correnti and Manin to petition the emperor for self-government and civil liberties. This was to be supported by a campaign encouraging abstention from smoking as a means of reducing Austrian tax revenue. In Milan it would lead to clashes with troops which proved to be decisive in the intensification of anti-Austrian feeling amongst the masses. By the beginning of 1848 if there was little thought anywhere in the Austrian Empire about revolution there was widespread and growing criticism of the regime and this was becoming increasingly embittered by the immobility of the central government[152, 156].

Some regimes had proved to be more responsive to pressures for change. In Britain, for a decade before 1848, a mass of propaganda had appeared in favour of such democratic reforms as manhood suffrage, the secret ballot, payment of Members of Parliament, equal electoral districts and annual Parliaments. Large numbers of people had come to believe that the establishment of such a democracy would lead to social reform. In terms of popular support, nothing in

Continental Europe could compare with Chartism. Even so, the circumstances in Britain were not conducive to revolution. Most notably a series of limited concessions, and particularly the 1832 Reform Act and the Repeal of the Corn Laws in 1846, combined with the fear of disorder and revolution induced by Chartism to reduce middle-class support for a radical politics[158, 164]. In Belgium the liberal electoral victory in 1847 was followed by a widening of the franchise with similar consequences. Elsewhere, as we have seen, governments were less willing to compromise. Aristocratic ministers were afraid that concessions would, as in France in 1789, only open the flood gates to further demands. In France Louis-Philippe and his prime minister Guizot were reassured by the solid governmental majority elected in 1846 and were confident that protest could be contained. In Prussia Friedrich Wilhelm IV was convinced of his Divine Right to rule, and confirmed in this by advisers drawn from the narrow circle of princes of the blood, and aristocratic civil and military officials. The dependence on the will of an individual and his advisers was a fundamental weakness of absolute monarchy. This was even more evident in Austria where a poorly educated and chronically ill ruler was incapable of imposing a sense of direction on his ministers, and where the Chancellor Metternich and Kolowrat the Interior Minister were rarely on speaking terms, and unable effectively to respond either to the increasingly desperate need to place the empire's finances on a sounder footing, or to pressures for reform. Thus Metternich, although aware of the deteriorating situation in Italy, failed to accept the recommendations of the Viceroy Fiquelmont in favour of reform or to exercise proper control over Radetzky, the military commander in Lombardy, who insisted late in 1847, with typical military presience, that with 'the whole social order . . . about to collapse . . . the Revolution will only be kept in check by fear'[145]. In practice, therefore, signs of growing discontent only confirmed the central government in its policy of preserving the status quo. It had lost touch with the reality of an Europe undergoing increasingly rapid economic and social change. In such circumstances the widespread failure of ruling elites to respond to pressures for change resulted in a growing political polarisation. Moreover, the combination of economic, social and political crisis caused a deepening loss of confidence amongst normal government supporters, increasing the likelihood of breakdown in a number of political systems[19].

3 'Revolution' as an Event

The widespread discontent so clearly evident in Europe at the beginning of 1848 was not in itself sufficient to cause a revolution. Very few people even considered the possibility of revolution. Why, then, in some areas, did conflict begin between representatives of the state and some of its subjects, and why in certain circumstances did this lead to *revolutionary situations*, that is, those in which a change of government occurred and in which the possibility of major social changes was at least in prospect? Why, moreover, was so much of the continent affected? Looking at the geography of revolution, one obvious point was that it began in capital cities – the foci for political activity, but also urban centres experiencing rapid economic change and population growth – and only subsequently affected other towns and rural areas. The outbreak in Paris on 23–24 February was clearly a major stimulant, everywhere serving to intensify governmental crises of confidence and to encourage opposition. Nevertheless the subsequent evolution of revolutionary situations depended primarily upon local and national circumstance.

In Paris the revolutionary outbreak was essentially spontaneous. The national campaign for electoral reform had been planned to culminate in a mass banquet in the city's 12th *arrondissement*. This, however, was banned by the government, anxious about the possibility of disorder. Liberals and moderate republicans accepted the ban but radicals called for a protest demonstration, and on 22 February crowds of students and workers gathered at the Madeleine and in the Place de la Concorde where sporadic violence occurred. The following day elements of the essentially middle-class National Guard (a civilian militia) made their support for reform clear, alienated as they were from a regime which seemed to represent solely the interests of the *grande bourgeoisie*. Louis-Philippe, his

35

confidence shaken, now accepted the need to make concessions and in the first place to replace Guizot with the more liberal Molé as prime minister. This essentially cosmetic move was well received by many middle-class supporters of reform, but in the poorer *quartiers* a small number of barricades appeared. Nevertheless, the crisis appeared to be subsiding, until around 10 p.m on the 23rd when a fusillade was fired, apparently without orders, by nervous troops guarding the Foreign Ministry in the Boulevard des Capucines. This enraged popular opinion. If, on the morning of 23 February, only a small minority of the population of the poor *quartiers* of the capital had been committed to the Republic, by early in the morning of the 24th some 1500 barricades had been constructed and a mass insurrection was underway against the king who murdered his people. In the narrow, tortuous streets of the old pre-Haussmann city, easily blocked by overturned carts, barrels and paving stones, bounded by tall buildings from which projectiles could be launched, the army tended to lose many of the advantages of discipline and fire power.

Marshal Bugeaud, notorious for his brutal repression of the 1834 republican insurrection, was instructed to crush this altogether more dangerous movement. He deployed four columns of troops with orders to clear the streets. However, it was difficult to use effectively troops who were untrained in street fighting. Without forceful leadership they tended to become demoralised easily. As a result, in the absence of clear governmental direction, and because of the lack of the support expected from the National Guard, Bugeaud's effort soon lost momentum, forcing him to withdraw his increasingly disorganised forces. This demoralised the king and his advisers to such a degree that Louis-Philippe was advised to abdicate, while members of the dynastic opposition, including Girardin, Thiers and Barrot, anxious to avoid a further deterioration in the political situation, attempted, with little success, to establish a regency in favour of the king's grandson. At the same time prominent republicans, meeting in the offices of their leading newspapers – the moderate *National*, and the more radical *Réforme* – and the anonymous secret society militants on the streets encouraged and sought to organise demands for a new, republican government. In the late afternoon, amongst scenes of great disorder and popular euphoria, a Provisional Government was proclaimed at the *Hôtel-de-Ville* made up of well-known parliamentarians and republican journalists[31, 36, 71]. Thus a revolution had occurred because, in a situation of economic and social crisis, the regime had lost the confidence of many of its habitual supporters. In response to a growing demand for political reform it had failed to introduce timely concessions. When an essentially fortuitous incident had led to a mass uprising it had been paralysed by a crisis of confidence and was unable to coordinate effective repression. As a result, a small body of active republicans had been able to take advantage of the regime's sudden loss of legitimacy to mobilise mass support in the capital, to seize power and establish a government. The very suddenness of this accession to power was to be the cause of future difficulties.

The news of events in France caused great excitement throughout Europe and encouraged the holding of public meetings and demonstrations – mainly involving the urban middle classes and skilled artisans – in favour of liberal reforms. A crisis rapidly built up within the Austrian Empire. On 3 March Kossuth was able to persuade a majority in the lower house of the Hungarian Diet, convened at Bratislava (Pressburg), to support a programme of constitutional reform designed to establish the autonomy of Hungary within the empire. On the same day 31 members of the Lower Austrian Estates meeting in Vienna called for the election of 'a patriotic and enlightened assembly' to advise the emperor on political reform. The proclamation issued on the following day by a group of officials and professional men, members of the Legal-Political Reading Club, was less restrained, however. It denounced 'the oppression of an absolute government', insisted upon the need to replace the Emperor's 'present counsellors' and on the reforms which it felt were necessary to restore confidence between the monarch and his people. These should establish a United Diet in which both the middle classes and the peasants would be represented; and to which ministers should be responsible; a more equitable taxation system; credit banks; legal reform; the expansion of education and the abolition of censorship. This was symptomatic of mounting agitation which caused great alarm in court circles. Initially, however, the emperor's advisers appear to have been determined to resist. Chancellor Metternich, while accepting the need for some change, insisted that this should be gradual, while Archduke Ludwig, President of the Council of State, recommended the strengthening of the Vienna garrison and the imposition of martial law.

In this tense situation a meeting of the Lower Austrian Diet on 13 March provided the occasion for the gathering of a large crowd. The subsequent development of events was similar to that in Paris. Troops ordered to clear the streets were met with a hail of missiles and eventually opened fire; in response demonstrators constructed barricades, partly to protect themselves, partly as a means of continuing the struggle. Middle-class Civil Guards refused to obey orders, and after two days of mounting disorder the emperor felt obliged to accept the resignation of Metternich, the symbol of the old order (who was replaced by his arch-rival Kolowrat, Interior Minister since 1825), and to promise a liberal constitution. On the 15th he also received a delegation from the Hungarian Diet and conceded greater autonomy to the Hungarians in the running of their own affairs[89, 143].

Events within the Hapsburg domains were developing rapidly. In a situation of governmental collapse it was inevitable that the subject peoples of the empire should seek to gain advantage. In Prague a petition to the emperor had been prepared on 11 March by a group meeting at St Václav's Baths composed mainly of Czech professional men, but including several Germans. Its suppliant, loyalist text entreated the ruler to introduce liberal measures[141]. Far more radical were developments in Italy, where the rulers of the independent states were forced to concede constitutions modelled on the French Charter of 1830. Here events were largely independent of those in France and Austria. The first of the European revolts had in fact taken place in Sicily, in Palermo, as early as 12 January. It had spread to the mainland of the Kingdom of Naples and forced Ferdinand II to grant a constitution on 29 January. He had been followed on 17 February by the Grand-Duke of Tuscany, on the 21st by the Pope and on 4 March by Charles-Albert of Piedmont – all anxious to avoid something worse. On 18 March, and this

38

time clearly inspired by the news from Paris and Vienna, a revolt against Austrian rule began in Milan. On that day a crowd of around 10,000 had presented a petition in favour of press freedom, the organisation of a citizens' militia and the election of a parliament. Again clashes with troops had occurred and barricades were constructed in the city centre. After five days of particularly bitter street fighting, Radetzky, the Austrian commander, who had remained inadequately prepared in spite of warnings from Vienna, was forced to withdraw his troops and retreat to the fortified belt known as the Quadrilateral, between Lake Como and the River Po. In Milan, although the records are incomplete, the insurgent dead included 107 artisans, 41 other workmen, 35 shopkeepers, clerks, etc., 12 peasants, 26 servants, 4 students, 3 apprentices, 16 *bourgeois* (merchants, landowners, etc.) and 4 children. Thirty-nine of them were women. As always, workers made up the majority of insurgents, but in Italy they were frequently reinforced by discontented peasants. Even more humiliating for the Austrians was the rapid capitulation of General Zichy in Venice. He had been discouraged by the lack of clear instructions from a government in Vienna which had sufficient problems of its own. Many of his troops were Italian and in the circumstances believed to be unreliable. His situation therefore seemed untenable. His surrender was followed on 17 March by the re-establishment of the Venetian republic with a provisional government led by Daniel Manin. This was followed by the withdrawal of Austrian garrisons from most of mainland Venetia, although significantly Verona, the key to the Brenner Pass, continued to be occupied[145, 150].

In Germany, too, where discontent was widespread, the news from France stimulated political demands. Disorders were reported from western Germany at the end of February, and had spread to Bavaria and East Prussia by the first week of March and into northern Germany including Berlin in the following week. Inevitably, in comparison with France, the political fragmentation of Germany resulted in a confused series of events. Yet, even if organised opposition parties did not exist, liberal and democratic leadership had already emerged in the press, in the various state diets and in the Prussian United Diet in 1847, which largely explains why events in every German capital took a similar course. At the same time widespread rural disorders occurred in the south-west, spreading into central Germany and to East Prussia. These represented the desire for the abolition of surviving feudal obligations, for the protection of traditional rights of usage on common land and in forests and for the condemnation of 'usury', the latter frequently made in anti-semitic terms. These movements, while obviously encouraged by the impending collapse of governmental authority and making it all the more likely, were otherwise unconnected with the more 'political' movements developing in the towns[83, 92, 130].

In a situation of deepening crisis conservatives in the smaller German states inevitably looked to Prussia and Austria for military support. This was not to be forthcoming. In Prussia Friedrich Wilhelm IV, faced with numerous petitions for reform, with serious urban and rural disorder, concerned about the uncertain attitude of the French Republic to its neighbours and above all by the news, received on 16 March, of the collapse of the Austrian regime, decided to make concessions. However, by the time these were announced on 18 March they already appeared belated and insufficient. As in Paris conflicting advice and indecision at the centre were leading to governmental collapse. On 18 March it was nevertheless decided to resist further pressure from demonstrating crowds in Berlin itself and military action caused over 200 civilian casualties, a majority of them skilled workers[100]. In the event its main effect was to provoke further protest, and on the morning of the 19th, in spite of the apparent success of the army in clearing barricades, the policy of repression was abandoned and the army ordered to leave the city. It was announced that the king had agreed to the establishment of a constitutional monarchy. This, together with the news from Vienna, helped ensure that similar concessions were made in the other German states, as their rulers turned to liberal politicians in the hope that they could contain the revolutionary menace and avoid something worse[89, 123].

The response of governments in Belgium and the Netherlands was similar. An effort was made to reduce discontent by means of the extension of voting rights and programmes of poor relief. In Britain, the Chartists had received the news from Paris with evident enthusiasm. A meeting in Halifax resolved that the French had: 'set an example worthy of imitation by all nations crushed beneath the tyrannical sway of Kingcraft, but more especially to those nations governed by a tyrannical oligarchy'[164]. In spite of this, and of the serious impact of European events upon the trade of London, Liverpool, Glasgow and the textile towns, most Chartist leaders would in the months which followed be unwilling to depart from their commitment to strictly legal agitation. Although briefly revitalised in 1848, their movement was already in decline and proved unable to mobilise sufficient support to pose a real threat to the established regime. Only in London, where the existence of a mass of small workshops and numerous underemployed building workers and general labourers replicated the social tension of Paris; in the Bradford area with its badly depressed worsted industry, and in Liverpool, was violence even contemplated and in all these areas Irish immigrants demanding repeal of the Union were to the fore. The government clearly benefited from divisions within the Chartist movement and its hesitant leadership. Another crucial factor was obvious official preparedness. Preventive measures involving the deployment of troops and police and the enrolment of special constables had the added advantage of increasing middle-class hysteria. However, premature repression which might have increased public sympathy for the Chartists was also avoided[161]. Then once convinced that the Chartist movement had been discredited and isolated by its exaggerated claims for support, by the numerous bogus signatures on its National Petition for reform, and by press publicity which blamed it for every minor disorder and chauvinistically took advantage of its association with Irish demands, in June the government felt able to arrest many of its local and national leaders[158, 159, 162].

At the opposite end of the developmental spectrum, in Russia, political liberalism had as yet very little support and was subject to effective authoritarian repression. In Spain, which might have appeared to be a likely candidate for revolution, with its narrowly based government, popular opposition and tradition of insurrection and military *pronunciamento*, and which was experiencing major economic distress,

41

only minor risings occurred in Madrid and Seville. For once the generals were relatively united in their fear of revolution[160].

European responses to complex situations of economic, social and political crisis were thus far from uniform. Where, as in Britain, legal constitutional change seemed possible, mass demonstrations in favour of reform were less likely to attract support, and when they did occur they did not constitute the sort of challenge to established authority which those in power felt had to be repressed with military force. The deployment of troops was all too likely to result in an upward cycle of violence, which only determined governments, confident of support from amongst at least the propertied classes, and in the capacity of their military power, could prevent. In 1848 a combination of poor leadership, division amongst the propertied classes, the loss of confidence within political elites, and the domino effect of governmental collapse, served to stimulate demands for reform and to discourage resistance[7].

4 Defining the Limits of Revolution: Post-revolutionary Conflict

The initial 'revolutions' took different forms in different states. These involved the violent overthrow of the monarchy in France, efforts to expel foreign rulers by force in Lombardy-Venetia or by constitutional means in Hungary, and an agreement to search for a constitutional compromise in the German States, Austria and Bohemia. To add to the complexity, the groups which had seized power or were seeking accommodation with the former authorities, were in effect coalitions. Both at the political centre and in numerous other localities, they were composed of people with differing and often conflicting objectives. The old regimes had collapsed so suddenly. Those who now claimed a share in political authority were surprised and unprepared. Events evolved so rapidly that they were never able to find time to take stock of their situation calmly. Certainly surprise had some advantages. Thus, outside the capital cities in which the political crises had come to a head, conservatives, including the military, were presented with a *fait accompli*. Although frightened by events, and especially by the prospect of social reforms, they tended grudgingly to accept changes in government in the absence of any obvious alternative. In general there was little opposition to the widespread assumption of central and local power by mainly liberal critics of previous regimes. However, it would become increasingly obvious in the months that followed that conservative elites had been merely biding their time.

In the immediate aftermath of revolution the pressing problems appeared to be to establish the membership and

43

authority of the new governments and to define constitutional settlements. How was the revolution to be consolidated? To what extent would previously quiescent groups now make political demands, encouraged by the weakening of central authority? Which of the diverse groups in contention would ultimately retain power? Would revolution once again lead to international war? For all these reasons, tension increased rather than diminished following the initial revolutionary success[25, 26].

In France, the Provisional Government which had emerged by popular acclaim was divided socially (7 of the 11 were wealthy notables and had been deputies during the July Monarchy – Dupont, Arago, Lamartine, Marie, Crémieux, Ledru-Rollin and Garnier-Pagès), personally and politically (Marie, Crémieux, Arago, Garnier-Pagès and Marrast were essentially liberals). They lacked governmental experience. These were men identified with opposition to the July Monarchy because of their participation in campaigns for franchise reform and their vague support for unspecified measures of social reform. They had sympathy for the poor, but like aristocratic and middle-class reformers elsewhere, they were unwilling or unable to contemplate changes which might alter the existing social system significantly. The majority saw their role as primarily one of preserving order and administrative continuity, and were anxious to keep their acts to a minimum until the election of a Constituent Assembly. Nevertheless, even these cautious men, in the circumstances, felt bound to accept such basic rights as manhood suffrage, freedom of speech, the press, and association, and the democratisation of the National Guard. These concessions, which increased the number of voters from 250,000 to close to 8 million, were likely to promote political mobilisation, with potentially disruptive consequences. Only a minority and most notably Ledru-Rollin, the socialist theoretician Blanc, and the worker Albert, advocated a more active policy of social reform. Thus the decree of 25 February which recognised the right to work, and established National Workshops, was intended simply to serve as a framework within which traditional forms of work relief could be provided for the unemployed. It was believed, however, by many workers to be only the first step in the

Organisation of Labour in producers' cooperatives along lines previously suggested by Blanc. Together with measures reducing the length of the working-day by one hour, abolishing the system of labour sub-contracting known as *marchandage*, and the establishment of the Luxembourg Commission, under Blanc's chairmanship, to enquire into working and living conditions, and to propose reforms, it created a sense of expectancy which it would prove dangerous to disappoint. It rapidly became clear that it was easier to agree on opposition to the monarchy than on positive measures of reform[40, 55].

Similar situations prevailed in Austria and the German States. In Prussia Friedrich Wilhelm had felt obliged to promise a constitution, and to consider electoral reform. To implement these measures two leading Rhineland liberals, Camphausen and Hansemann, were appointed ministers. On another key issue – greater German unity – the king was too concerned to preserve his own and his fellow princes' rights to risk taking the initiative[95]. However, the matter was not allowed to rest. In a genuinely revolutionary act, on 5 March, 51 liberals from western and southern Germany, meeting at Heidelberg, elected a committee of seven charged with convoking a gathering of the members of existing state assemblies at Frankfurt. On 30 March, 600 of these agreed to form a Pre-Parliament (*Vorparlament*) which determined that national elections should be held to elect an assembly whose function would be to prepare a German constitution, that it should be elected, on the basis of one deputy for every 50,000 inhabitants, by voters whose essential qualification should be 'independence', that is, property ownership, although the individual states would be left to establish their own electoral systems. The latter point was symptomatic of an unwillingness to risk a breach with the existing authorities and of a continuing dependence upon the bureaucratic and military organisations which these authorities still controlled. With the exception of a small radical minority, the supporters of constitutional reform wanted to proceed by means of compromise, through 'agreement' with legally constituted authority. This understandable reluctance to provoke further violence left considerable room for manoeuvre to the monarchs and traditional elites, although in the short term further concessions to reform

45

would prove to be necessary as a result of the widespread political mobilisation provoked by the revolutions[106].

In each of the states affected by revolution, this had created a situation in which diverse groups felt able to make demands and seek recognition of vital interests. In many communities this was stimulated by local political factionalism, as members of prominent families sought to take advantage of a fluid political situation in order to secure administrative office as a means of increasing their status and influence. The creation of clubs and discussion groups, and of newspapers representing a variety of political options was the most obvious manifestation of this competition for local and national power. It was sustained longest in the larger cities but occurred in most areas and served to encourage political activity by workers and peasants by both direct influence and processes of imitation. This mass involvement was particularly pronounced where existing community social networks, as well as organisations such as mutual aid societies, promoted a sense of solidarity and facilitated action. In Paris, at their peak the political clubs had some 100,000 members, and workers' associations around 40,000. These only institutionalised a ferment which spread into the *cafés* and streets. There was also widespread, if sporadic, disorder. Workers protested about unemployment and low wages[32, 42, 47]. Peasants complained about taxation and restrictions on access to common land and forests and other features of the growth of capitalistic farming. In Alsace and south-west Germany they denounced Jewish 'usurers', and in other parts of Germany and Austria surviving feudal restrictions. The era of 'freedom' appeared to have dawned. Abstract and universalistic political principles were reinterpreted by various groups in terms of their own immediate interests, and in a fashion which frequently revealed a deep, and hitherto normally concealed, aversion for the social order. More widespread disorder thus occurred in the aftermath of the Revolution than during the actual revolutionary events themselves, although these movements of protest, lacking formal organisation and a programme, usually ceased of their own accord. As a result the new liberal administrations frequently were forced to employ the existing state apparatus to restore order.

This all added to a growing sense of uncertainty, with adverse consequences for business confidence and levels of activity. As a result, revolution led to renewed economic crisis. Those liberals who had assumed governmental power, or at least, as in most German states, had been granted a share in authority, were thus faced with a complex of serious problems. They were expected to take measures to alleviate the social difficulties caused by the crisis and to limit the risks of further disorder. At the same time they were involved in complex debates on constitutional reform, in which, initially at least, they were anxious to conciliate both radicals and conservatives and to limit the possibility of either further revolution or counter-revolution[55, 123].

In France the Provisional Government, while accepting the need for such stop-gap measures as the National Workshops to provide work-relief for the unemployed, was primarily concerned to promote business confidence as the means of restoring prosperity. This required the maintenance of public order and the avoidance of 'socialistic' measures. The first objective, together with the possibility of foreign intervention against the revolution, established the republican regime's dependence upon the military, and ensured that a far-reaching purge of the officer corps would not occur. As many as 50,000 troops were rapidly deployed in rural areas to repress disorders caused mainly by long-standing disputes over collective rights of usage on agricultural land and in forests (particularly in upland areas of the east and Pyrenees). Peasant expectations of sympathetic treatment by the new government were further disabused by the decree of 16 March which established an extraordinary increase of 45 per cent in direct taxation (mainly on land)[37]. This reflected the government's concern to balance the budget and meet the costs of the National Workshops. Comprehensible as a means of increasing business confidence, it was not the way to win peasant support for the Republic[40, 47]! Throughout the German states also, governments and municipalities tried to minimise unrest by expanding work-relief programmes. In contrast with France, a series of measures were proposed which would have the effect of reducing peasant discontent even if legislation on this and other matters was postponed until meetings of state diets

47

and the Frankfurt Parliament. Thus surviving seigneural rights were to be attenuated or abolished, giving peasants greater control over the land they cultivated, although demands from the landless for the sub-division of common land were ignored[102]. In Austria too, a series of measures (culminating in a general law of 7 September 1848) conceded the abolition of feudal obligations and effectively demobilised the peasantry[83, 92].

The intense political debate so characteristic of these early months of 1848 served to widen divisions amongst liberals and between them and the supporters of political democracy and social reform. It was already evident that if there was widespread support for change there was no common vision of its nature. In east Prussia, for example, the prestigious newspaper, the *Königsberger Zeitung*, with its 3900 subscribers, wanted parliamentary government with increased opportunities for the gifted and successful members of the middle classes to participate in politics, but firmly opposed extending the franchise to the uneducated and politically immature masses. It also denied that the State was under any obligation to provide public assistance, and insisted that Prussia must retain its autonomy within a future united Germany[114]. These views were representative of a liberalism which opposed social reform, of middle classes increasingly frightened by what they saw as the growing 'insolence' of the working classes and terrified at the prospect of further revolution engineered by those Camphausen called the *Kommunistencliquen*[119]. They were to be increasingly willing to accept the use of the military to repress every threat – real or imagined – to the sanctity of private property. The democratic *Neue Königsberger Zeitung*, founded during the summer of 1848, challenged these views but failed to attract more than 500 subscribers.

Rising social tension was especially evident in Berlin where a multitude of new newspapers, pamphlets, associations and political clubs sought to influence the population. Most notable, on the left, were the republican and social newspaper, *Die Zeitungshalle*, and the even more radical *Volksfreund* with its demands for the division of large estates amongst the poor and calls for class war. The printing worker Stefan Born, a close associate of Marx and Engels in the Communist League, played an influential role in organising a workers' club and a Workers' Central Committee. He insisted that, while workers needed to press for an improvement of their own conditions and to secure the right to work, state credits for producers' cooperatives, and better opportunities for education, in the prevailing circumstances they depended upon an alliance with the *bourgeoisie* against the aristocracy and monarchy and should take care not to frighten the middle classes. Nevertheless as the economic situation deteriorated, unrest grew and was intensified by such measures as the exclusion of workers from the new civil guard (the *Bürgerwehr*)[76, 88, 112].

These divisions were represented amongst the delegates who met in the Paulskirche at Frankfurt on 18 May to prepare a German constitution. The combination of restricted franchises (excluding 10–25 per cent of adult males), systems of indirect election, and mass indifference, together with the superior education and organisational capacity of the middle classes, had resulted in the election (as in France) of an assembly dominated by jurists and officials[90, 121]. (At its maximum the members included 1 peasant, 4 artisans, 11 clerks, 60 landowners, 80 businessmen, 106 professors, 223 lawyers, 118 senior officials and 116 without profession.) Even so, the simultaneous election of state and national parliaments undoubtedly contributed to the process of politicisation. At Frankfurt parliamentary factions soon developed. The so-called Party of the Casino (named after its meeting place), that is, the centre-right liberals, with Heinrich von Gagern, a Hessian noble, as their leading figure, emerged as the strongest single group. To its right were the particularist and reactionary conservatives who gathered in the café Milani. The centre-left liberals met in the Württemberger Hof and Augsburger Hof. They were dominated by southerners suspicious of Prussian intentions, and with some sympathy for notions of popular sovereignty. The 47 republicans ensconced in the Donnersberg, and the small democratic and socialist group led by Robert Blum meeting at the Deutscher Hof were on the far left[105, 124].

The members of the Assembly were determined to assert what they believed to be their rights. They rapidly established a responsible ministry under an Imperial Vicar (*Reichsverweser*), realistically selecting the Austrian Archduke John, a man acceptable to both the Austrian and Prussian monarchs. They additionally voted the creation of a national army and fleet. However, fundamental divisions of principle between them were already evident over such matters as whether or not to include Austria with its non-German peoples within the new German Empire[131, 132], on the question of the franchise, and on the possibility of social reform. Political differences were reinforced by religious and social distinctions. Surprisingly, given the widespread repugnance for democracy, and probably due to an inability to agree on an alternative, a law would eventually emerge, on 12 April 1849, accepting something close to manhood suffrage. By that time the Assembly was close to dissolution anyway[84, 90]. More characteristic was the work of the Assembly's Economic Committee. It considered a large volume of evidence, and proposed measures which would, if implemented, have had the effect of reducing guild restrictions on individual enterprise. In a statement redolent with self-satisfaction, it rejected the sort of guarantee of work made by the Provisional Government in France on the grounds that: 'such a guarantee would be the paralysis of diligence, a sanction of laziness'. It saw its 'duty', rather, as 'to reinforce the trust in their strength of those classes on which the Providence of God has imposed labour as a necessity of life'[79, 99].

It quickly became evident that the implementation of any of these measures depended upon the good will of the major states, and that the Assembly relied in particular upon their military support. This was made clear in September 1848, when a republican-inspired uprising, in protest against the failure to annex the Danish provinces of Schleswig and Holstein, took place in Frankfurt itself, and a group of exiles crossed the Baden frontier and attempted to proclaim a republic. In April 1849 agreement was finally reached on constitutional proposals which included the establishment of a federal union with an elected diet, a responsible ministry and an emperor with substantial executive power. But by then, Friedrich Wilhelm, the most favoured candidate, was determined not to accept the imperial crown at the hands of an elected assembly. In this situation the majority of delegates, aware of the weakness of their position and anxious to avoid disorder, were unwilling to attempt to enforce a solution[90]. The Assembly had lost all credibility. Following the recall of Austrian and Prussian delegates it was dissolved on 30 May. This failure on the part of the liberal *bourgeoisie*, and its overwhelming concern with the preservation of order rather than its political rights, has represented for historians one of the 'peculiarities of German history'[81, 94], although within the context of 1848 an ambivalent attitude towards 'liberty' was anything but unique.

The history of the Frankfurt Assembly itself suggests that historians have not given sufficient attention to political developments at the level of the individual German states. In most of them similar patterns of development were evident, however[85]. In Prussia, by far the most important politically and in terms of its population, on 2 April 1848 the Camphausen–Hansemann government had reluctantly presented to the United Diet a proposal granting the vote to all men over 24 (with indirect election as a means of limiting its democratic impact), for the election of an assembly which would discuss constitutional questions with the king. The Diet, dominated by the old elites, but resigned to reform ('terrorised' according to Bismarck) also confirmed the concessions already made by the king on such matters as freedom of the press and assembly, the equal treatment of Protestants and Catholics, and parliamentary control over the budget. The new assembly elected early in May was significantly different in its social composition from that meeting at Frankfurt. It included 178 officials and lawyers (but generally of modest rank), 49 peasants (and only 24 big landowners), 28 artisans, 50 clergymen and 27 schoolmasters. Politically it too was dominated by liberals, but with a larger and more active group of radicals. Hansemann, who replaced Camphausen as the dominant figure in the ministry in late June, was determined to reshape the Prussian state in order to reduce noble power and proposed the ending of noble tax privileges and the curtailment of their local administrative and judicial authority. In October the assembly went so far as to vote the abolition of such fundamental symbols of Prussian society as the formula 'King, by the Grace of God' and titles of nobility –

51

measures which inevitably stimulated a powerful reaction, supported by the king, who made his unwillingness to accept the status of a constitutional monarch clear by his intervention in government, especially in military matters. The passage of time revealed a growing loss of confidence amongst liberals due in particular to their fear of popular unrest, and a renewal of confidence in court circles seen in the appointment of increasingly conservative ministers and the imposition of a constitution in December by the Manteuffel ministry without the assembly's agreement. In the circumstances this was surprisingly liberal, preserving universal male suffrage and ministerial responsibility to parliament but additionally insisting upon the king's right to veto legislation, and the possibility of rule by decree[95, 96].

In March 1848, under pressure from the streets, liberal concessions had also been made in Austria. These included the promise to reform the police and central administration, and to establish parliamentary government. On 25 April it was announced that a bicameral parliament would be created with a lower chamber to be elected on a restricted franchise, and an upper chamber composed of large landowners and members appointed by the emperor. The monarch would moreover retain the right to veto all legislation. This provoked further demonstrations in Vienna on 15 May which secured the concession of voting rights for all males, over 24, who were 'independently employed' and a single, elected chamber. This Imperial Chamber would meet for the first time on 22 July; 60 per cent of its 383 members would be *bourgeois*, 25 per cent peasants, and the remainder mainly clergy and nobles; 190 Slav deputies were elected. The political inexperience of most of its members and the bitter divisions of interest which distinguished them meant that it achieved very little.

While making such major concessions to urban protest, the dominant figures within frequently changing ministries, made up largely of senior civil servants – men such as Kolowrat, Fiquelmont and Pillersdorf – appear to have been even more afraid of rural insurrection, bearing in mind the violent Galician uprisings in 1846. Thus a decree of 28 March abolished labour service (the *robot*) and other feudal obligations. This was later confirmed by parliament, and was sufficient to satisfy most peasants. Subsequently within Austria itself (excluding Hungary and Italy) the essential problem for the emperor and his advisers would be to contain middle-class liberalism and radicalism. In Vienna this manifested itself in the dangerous form of an expansion of the armed civic guard and the creation by students of an Academic Legion. The authorities also sought to prevent the development of popular demonstrations like that of 15 May, after which the royal family had secretly left the capital for the greater security of Innsbruck, a move which symbolised the threat of 'republican anarchy'.

There and in other towns in the German-speaking provinces such as Linz and Graz, citizens' committees had assumed control over local government. But it could be assumed that these bodies would cooperate in the preservation of public order and prevent the recurrence of the attacks on food shops and the burning of tax registers which had marked the early stages of the revolution. In effect, once concessions to liberal demands had been made, a political realignment had commenced. The more moderate, especially amongst the better-off and economically secure upper and middle, middle classes (landowners, officials, business and professional men) affirmed their fundamental desire to avoid social change, and their willingness to preserve a strong, protective monarchy[89, 143]. This indeed was the general pattern of response throughout Europe to the development of demands for radical political and social change.

Such demands had obviously been encouraged by the relaxation of normal repressive pressures. Radical mobilisation was now to be most effective where *bourgeois* professionals skilled at communication and political organisation allied with groups of craftsmen, and in some areas with peasants, who possessed shared values and basic organisational structures associated with their trades and forms of community sociability, together with the desire to defend their livelihoods against growing commercial pressures[4]. Through these links existing grievances might increasingly be combined with explicit political claims. Although it is not likely that more than a small minority of workers and peasants developed a modern conception of politics based upon an awareness of institutions and ideology, the new liberties and sense of expectancy led, particularly in the towns, to discussion, organisation and propaganda which accelerated the processes of politicisation[72]. It was in France that the growth of this radical politics first led to a renewed revolutionary outburst and to the onset of political reaction.

In Paris, which remained the key to the future of the revolution in France, the worker cooperations and the popular clubs had revived the political societies of the first revolution. The discourse in clubs such as Auguste Blanqui's *Société républicaine centrale* or Barbès' *Club de la révolution* was frequently extreme. The manifesto of the latter announced that: 'we still only have the name of the Republic, we need the real thing. Political reform is only the instrument of social reform'. These radical groups were determined to press the Provisional Government for immediate social reform. The sudden sense of liberation and awakening of political life was thus translated into continuing pressure upon the government from radicals and workers determined to avoid a repetition of what was regarded as the betrayal of 1830. Major demonstrations took place on 17 March (with 150,000–200,000 participants) on 16 April and 15 May. To further these aims on 20 March the delegates of around 60 Parisian clubs agreed on the establishment of a joint *Club des clubs* which ultimately dispatched 300–500 organisers into the provinces. There, too, numerous – mainly short-lived – clubs (both radical and conservative) were organised, and everyday life became more politicised than before. In cities such as Lyon, democratic organisation was based upon an existing structure of secret societies. It seems clear that workers were already more politicised before 1848 than they had been in 1830. Typically these clubs had a mixed middle-class and working-class membership with middle-class leadership. They contributed to the popularising of demands for social reform through such slogans as the *Organisation du travail* and the *République démocratique et sociale*. This, together with the violence of their language, frightened conservatives and contributed substantially to the increase of social tension[32, 55, 62].

Many radicals had assumed that the election of a Constituent Assembly by universal male suffrage would ensure a majority committed to social reform. However, although radical candidates attracted considerable support amongst the relatively politicised urban lower-middle and working classes, in the countryside, in which most electors lived, conservative propaganda tended to be better organised and, with its stress on the restoration of social order as the only means of re-establishing prosperity, to possess greater appeal. Faced with a plethora of candidates, inexperienced voters often turned for help to their traditional advisers, to those who enjoyed the status and social power conveyed by wealth and education or function, including the clergy. Indeed one result of the establishment of universal male suffrage was to establish a clear concordance between conservative voting and religious commitment, in opposition to what was perceived to be a challenge to the eternal values of religion as well as to social order. In Flanders, and the west and south-west, socio-religious factors were often more influential than class differences. Where influence did not suffice, intimidation was commonly employed. The poor needed to be prudent. Many rural voters no doubt soon subsided into indifference once it seemed clear that the Republic would do little to change their situation and indeed was intent upon increasing taxes. Others remained convinced that the Republic threatened their property and sought security in voting for candidates who promised protection against those who, it was claimed, planned to redistribute the land, the so-called *partageux*. Democratic republicans had little time to combat this.

Assessment of the results of the April 1848 elections is difficult in the absence of organised parties, and due to the appearance of many candidates on the lists of a number of apparently incompatible political persuasions; and where virtually all candidates called themselves republicans and presented extremely vague political programmes. Nevertheless, three basic groups can be identified: conservatives, moderates and radicals. The first two groups tended to stress their respect for the family, property and religion, and the need to restore social order. Moderate republicans were basically satisfied by the political changes introduced by the Provisional Government. The last group insisted on the need

55

for social reforms which should include recognition of the right to work and state intervention in the economy to ensure this. Its members usually, at the same time, tried to assure conservatives that the revolution of 1848 was not going to be like the Terror of 1793.

The membership of the Constituent Assembly made it likely that a clash would occur – and sooner rather than later – with those groups, particularly in Paris, which had seen the revolution as inaugurating a new era, in which the rights of the working man (to employment, a decent wage, and self-respect) would be recognised. Only a minority of the nearly 900 deputies elected appear to have been republicans before 1848 (about 300), and only 70–80 of these would evince any clear sympathy for substantial measures of social reform. The remainder were monarchists, most of whom temporarily adopted a republican label (including probably 5 Bonapartists and 56 Legitimists, 19 former supporters of Guizot, 231 representatives of the former dynastic opposition, 133 monarchists whose dynastic loyalties are unknown, and 122 whose options are uncertain, but mainly monarchist). Socially this was to be an assembly of wealthy provincial notables. These included landowners and especially representatives of the traditional *bourgeois* professions: 261 members of the liberal professions, including 176 lawyers; about 170 public officials; 170 members of the economic professions including 24 wage-earners; 279 with professions unknown, but mainly large landowners (*propriétaires*). The political inexperience of most of its members made it relatively easy for experienced parliamentarians, mainly liberals from the dynastic left and centre-left of the July Monarchy, to assume leading roles through their rhetorical skills, organisation of a caucus (by the Comité de la rue de Poitiers) and control of parliamentary committees. Indeed complementary elections in June saw the return to the Assembly of such Orleanist leaders as Molé and most notably Thiers[31, 33].

The growing disillusionment of Parisian radicals with this situation was made clear on 15 May when crowds demonstrating in favour of support for the Polish rebellion against Russian rule broke through National Guard cordons around the Constituent Assembly, entered the building and demanded both French military intervention in Eastern Europe and immediate measures to provide workers with work and food. Taking advantage of the situation, some militants, most notably Huber and Sobrier, sought to establish a committee of public safety with unlimited powers and the declared aim of levying an extraordinary tax on the wealthy to finance the creation of producers' cooperatives. This attempted coup was quickly suppressed. It appears to have been unplanned and the crowds were unarmed. It was followed by the arrest not only of those most involved but of other radicals including Blanqui, Raspail, Barbès and the former minister Albert, together with the closure of some political clubs. Significantly too, the proceedings of the Luxembourg Commission were terminated and its proposals for reform never discussed. May 15 furthermore strengthened the conservative alliance committed to the restoration of 'normality' and accelerated the polarisation of political opinion in Paris[55]. Although the Executive Commission elected by the Constituent Assembly was to reaffirm its commitment to such measures as tax reform and the provision of cheap credit as well as to the nationalisation of the railways and assurance companies, its primary concern was to be with the maintenance of public order. This forced it into growing dependence upon the well-organised conservative groups in the Assembly. These increasingly focused their attention upon the National Work-shops which both served as the symbol of revolution and were an expensive, an increasingly politicised and a potentially dangerous organisation of workers[33, 36].

Tension grew night after night, with large gatherings in the streets listening to extreme republicans and also Bonapartist agitators, until dispersed by the police. Although apparently established to implement the Provisional Government's com-mitment to the right to work the National Workshops had proved a disappointment. They provided hard and often pointless physical labour for minimal rewards. Rather than serving as the first in a network of producers' cooperatives employing workers in their own trades they resembled nothing more than the traditional charity workshop. Throughout the 1840s socialists had discussed cooperation and for as long as

57

the Workshops existed this dream of social reform remained alive. Their existence, however, came increasingly into question in the Constituent Assembly. As a result, as police reports revealed, workers became increasingly disillusioned with legal political processes. Finally, on 22 June, it was announced that the National Workshops were to be closed. Workers aged 17 to 25 were to be given the option of enlisting in the army, and the others were promised employment on public works in the provinces. A delegation of workers led by a man called Pujol was told, with amazing lack of tact, by Marie on behalf of the Executive Commission, that: 'if the workers do not want to leave, we will send them from Paris by force'. No effort was made to reassure the tens of thousands of unemployed that poor relief provision would be made for them. These words, reported to crowds on the Place du Luxembourg and then at the Place de la Bastille, convinced many that with such an uncaring government there was no alternative but *recommencer la Révolution*. They had believed that the Republic would improve their lives by guaranteeing employment, now their last hope was being denied them. They felt that they were being betrayed by the regime they had themselves created in February. On the 23rd, following further mass meetings at the Panthéon and the Bastille, again addressed by Pujol and inspired by his slogan 'Liberty or Death!' an essentially spontaneous revolt began, by which Paris was clearly cut into two parts, with barricades being constructed essentially in the poorer, eastern *quartiers*. Leadership gradually emerged at local level from amongst the better-known club militants. Weapons were seized from gunsmiths and private homes; many already possessed National Guard equipment. Indeed, the basic organisational framework for the struggle in most districts was the neighbourhood military organisation of the Guard. There was, however, no overall plan, no collective leadership emerged, and the insurrection very rapidly became nothing more than a desperately fought defence of isolated neighbourhoods.

Information derived from the lists of people arrested indicates that the insurgents were drawn mainly from the small-scale artisanal trades of the city, such as building, metalwork, clothing and shoes, and furniture, with the addition of some workers from modern industrial establishments such as the railway engineering workshops, as well as a large number of unskilled labourers and a not inconsiderable group of small businessmen. These were not rootless vagabonds as was often claimed by conservative propagandists but mostly skilled workers, well-integrated into their crafts and neighbourhood communities. It was the strength of these loyalties which explained high levels of participation in such *arrondissements* as the 6th, 9th and 12th. Each of the main centres of resistance was dominated by particular trades – carters at La Villette, dock workers along the St-Martin canal, bronze workers in the Boulevard du Temple, joiners and cabinet makers in the Faubourg St-Antoine.

Estimates of the numbers engaged vary. Possibly 40,000–50,000 were involved to some degree. Many workers stayed at home, others continued to earn a wage in the National Workshops, although a significant number of men from the Workshops did take to the barricades. Some fought on the other side. Nevertheless a substantial number of men and some women were sufficiently disappointed with the outcome of the revolution to risk their lives in an attempt to establish a more democratic and reformist republic. They felt that they were fighting for justice[55, 63].

Against them were ranged the forces of 'order'. These consisted of National Guard units from the wealthier western *quartiers*, made up of property owners, shopkeepers, clerks, professional men and intellectuals and workers. They were anxious to defend their own neighbourhoods and to affirm their commitment to an ordered, hierarchical society and to crush the threatened social revolution, the prospect of 'anarchy' as they saw it. Political differences were forgotten. Although many workers failed to report for duty with the National Guard, they still made up about one-fifth of the Guards committed against the insurrection. Many of them, like the mason from the Creuse, Martin Nadaud, saw the insurrection as a threat to the republic. He represented the agonising dilemma of many republicans when he wrote that:

our hearts [are] torn apart by bitter distress and our agony

Participation in the insurrection of June 1848: professions of those arrested

Profession	No. arrested	Total arrested %
Building	1,725	14.82
Food and drink	438	3.76
Furniture	1,004	8.62
Clothing and shoes	1,225	10.52
Textiles	351	3.01
Skin and leather	157	1.35
Coach building, saddlery and military equipment	223	1.92
Chemicals and ceramics	116	1.00
Metal, engineering and metal products	1,312	11.27
Precious metals and jewellery	231	1.98
Coopers and basket-makers	68	0.58
Printing workers	433	3.72
Labourers and navvies	1,093	9.39
Cultivators, gardeners and herdsmen	141	1.21
Transport workers	522	4.48
Concièrges, servants, cooks and waiters	282	2.42
Proprietors, *rentiers*	47	0.40
Clerical workers	438	3.76
Liberal professions	208	1.79
Artistic professions	72	0.62
Commercial professions (including shopkeepers)	450	3.77
Students	39	0.33
Garde mobile	163	1.40
Police and soldiers	216	1.86
Ragpickers, pedlars, etc.	297	2.55
Others	297	2.56
Occupation not specified	94	0.81
	11,642	99.90

Source: Roger Price, *The French Second Republic* (Batsford, 1972), p. 165.

is cruel. On the side of the people, there are terrible grievances of suffering and despair; there are accumulated grudges which are for the most part legitimate. On the side of the republic there is our essential principle, the great principle of the republic, and whatever the faults of individuals might be, there has been no violation by the government of sovereign rights.

This stance was to isolate other radicals, such as Ledru-Rollin, from the Parisian workers. A major role in the fighting was given to the *gardes mobiles*. They were organised from amongst young, unemployed workers after February. Their loyalties remained in doubt until the last minute, but because of their youth, they were not as yet integrated into craft and neighbourhood communities, and so they remained loyal to their comrades and to the government which paid them[65]. Most important of all, however, in the work of repression, was the regular army which was to become in the eyes of the propertied classes, the 'saviour of civilisation'. Overall command was placed in the hands of General Cavaignac, Minister of Defence, who was asked on the 24th by the Constituent Assembly to replace the discredited Executive Commission as head of government.

Cavaignac, anxious to avoid a repetition of February, when dispersed groups of troops had been overwhelmed, was determined to concentrate his forces. This took time and had serious consequences. Apparent military inaction encouraged the insurgents. It enabled them to persuade and coerce reluctant participants, and to extend the network of barricades. However, once concentration had been achieved, the rising was smashed in three days of bitter street fighting, followed by 12,000 arrests (many due to anonymous denunciations) which decimated the Parisian left for a decade. The artist Meissonier, a National Guard captain, described the violence of civil war: 'when the barricade in the rue de la Mortellerie was taken, I realised all the horror of such warfare. I saw the defenders shot down, hurled out of windows, the ground strewn with corpses, the earth red with blood'[37, 43, 49].

Whatever the precise sociological character of the conflict,

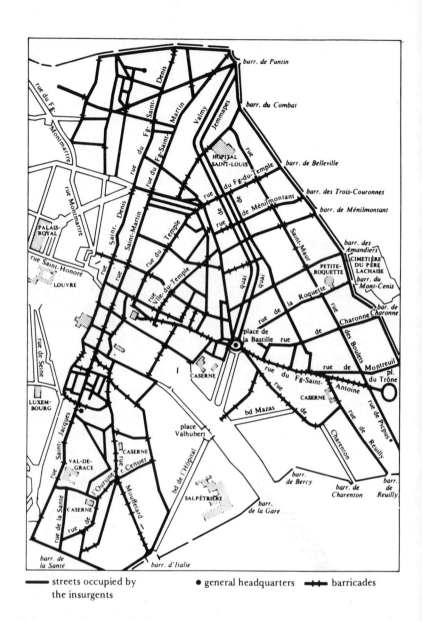

Map labels:

barr. de Puntin

barr. du Combat

HÔPITAL SAINT-LOUIS

barr. de Belleville

barr. des Trois-Couronnes

barr. de Ménilmontant

barr. des Amandiers

CIMETIÈRE DU PÈRE LACHAISE

barr. du Mont-Cenis

barr. de Charonne

PETITE-ROQUETTE

place de la Bastille

rue du Fg-Saint-Antoine

CASERNE

pl. du Trône

rue de Montreuil

rue de Picpus

rue de Reuilly

bd Mazas

place Valhubert

VAL-DE-GRÂCE

CASERNE

r. Censier

SALPÊTRIÈRE

barr. de la Gare

barr. de Bercy

barr. de Charenton

barr. de Reuilly

barr. de la Santé

barr. d'Italie

LUXEM-BOURG

PALAIS-ROYAL

LOUVRE

rue Saint-Honoré

rue de Seine

rue de la Santé

rue Saint-Jacques

l'Oursine

Mouffetard

bd de l'Hôpital

CASERNE

Saint-Denis

Saint-Martin

rue du Temple

rue Vile-du-Temple

rue du Fg-Saint-Martin

rue du Fg-Saint-Denis

Valmy

Jemmapes

rue du Fg-du-Temple

de Ménilmontant

Saint-Maur

de la Roquette

quai

des Boulets

rue du Fg. Montmartre

Montmartre

rue Montmartre

—— streets occupied by the insurgents • general headquarters ✚✚ barricades

Map VII   Insurgent Paris in June 1848.
Source: M. Agulhon, *The Republican Experiment, 1848–1852* (Cambridge University Press, 1983)

62

contemporaries saw it as one between *bourgeois* and *peuple*, as a form of class struggle. According to de Tocqueville, the insurrection was a:

> brutal, blind but powerful attempt by the workers to escape from the necessities of their condition, which had been described to them as an illegitimate oppression . . . It was this mixture of cupidity and false theory which rendered the insurrection so formidable . . . These poor people had been assured that the well-being of the rich was in some way based upon theft from themselves.

The conservative press depicted the events as an outbreak of extreme savagery, as a rising fought for nothing more than 'pillage and rape'[64].

News of the outbreak in Paris spread gradually into the provinces. There were some demonstrations of sympathy, and Marseille experienced a minor insurrection on 22–23 June. Such incidents tended to be seen by the authorities as signs of a widespread plot, centred on Paris, to destroy the existing social system. The overwhelming response in the provinces, however, was mobilisation to defend social order. Even before the Paris insurrection had been crushed, National Guard volunteers from the provinces were marching to the aid of the army. In Lyon the opportunity was taken to disarm suspect National Guardsmen[48, 62]. Above all else, however, the effect of the June Days was to heighten social fear. The initial cry of triumph at the 'victory gained by the cause of order, of the family, of humanity, of civilisation' (*Journal des Débats*, 1 July) was followed by demands from conservatives and many erstwhile moderate republicans for thoroughgoing political reaction. For the latter insurrection represented an intolerable attack on the popular sovereignty represented by the Constituent Assembly. Many of them were ready to join other *notables*, whatever their political views, against the common danger. Together these *notables*, through their economic and social power and position in the administration, army and press, were able to exert overwhelming influence[66].

This crushing defeat imposed upon the revolution in Paris provided a powerful stimulus to reaction not only in France, but throughout Europe. The tide appeared to be turning. This was the view of both de Tocqueville and Marx, each of whom wrote a powerful analysis of the events of June. Their views have exercised a substantial influence on writing about revolution by both historians and sociologists ever since[16, 64].

Rather than marking the end of pressure for further revolution, however, these events shifted the focus of the radical movement away from Paris and into the provinces, with the development by democrats and socialists of such propaganda organisations as *Solidarité républicaine* from the autumn of 1848. The elections held in May 1849 revealed a major shift in opinion, and especially, a remarkable degree of political polarisation. The moderate republicans were reduced to 75–80 deputies, while the number of radicals (Montagnards or *démocrate-socialistes*) had risen to around 200, elected not only in the working-class *quartiers* of the major cities, but also in rural areas, especially in the south-east. To a large degree, this was due to the success of the left in linking their political programme to the pressing problems caused by the depression affecting agriculture and rural industry[52, 55]. The apparent defection of peasants to the 'reds', and the threat which this posed to social stability, impressed public opinion more than the election of 500 conservative deputies. A major effort had been made by middle-class radicals resident in major and minor market centres to penetrate their rural hinterlands, encouraging organisation, and distributing propaganda in the form of songs, pamphlets and newspapers. These promised the right to work, free education, support for the establishment of producers' and consumers' cooperatives, cheap credit and reduced taxation for the poor, to be paid for by higher taxes on the rich and the nationalisation of key sectors of the economy. Especially in areas with a high proportion of relatively independent peasant proprietors, living in large villages with good communications linking them to neighbouring market (and political) centres, the ability to offer what appeared to be practical solutions to pressing problems secured mass support for the left[30, 34, 51].

This advance by the left in the provinces led to an intensification of the repressive governmental pressures already evident following the June Days[54]. It was reinforced after the election of Louis-Napoléon Bonaparte as President of the Republic in December 1848[67]. In order to survive *démocrate-socialiste* groups were increasingly forced underground, and became in effect secret societies, often employing such traditional folkloric manifestations as carnival and the *charivari* (a traditional form of protest by members of a community against someone who had offended against its norms of behaviour – employing ribald songs and discordant music made by banging on saucepans, kettles, etc.), to express openly their hostility to local conservatives[35]. Finally, there was a massive wave of social protest in December 1851, in response to news of Bonaparte's *coup d'état* which seemed to threaten once and for all the prospect of social reform which the left still believed would follow victory in the general elections due to be held in 1852. These protests were especially strong in parts of the centre and south-east. Economic difficulties, although a major cause of unrest, did not in any deterministic sense lead to involvement in this insurrection. However, for many poor people *1852*, and the creation of the *République démocratique et sociale*, had represented the only possible means of escaping from poverty, insecurity and misery, and of asserting their desire for a more egalitarian community. The naïvety of their beliefs does not detract from the depth of their commitment. The new era of human happiness which had been promised by *démo-soc* militants, by republicans with a faith in progress and the triumph of democracy, was worth struggling for.

Some 100,000 men from around 900 communes were involved; as many as 70,000 from at least 775 communes actually took up arms in these disturbances and over 27,000 participated in acts of violence. Armed insurrection occurred in the centre (Allier, Nièvre), south-west (Lot-et-Garonne, Gers) and especially the south-east (Drôme, Ardèche, Basses-Alpes, Hérault, Var), that is in a minority of rural areas south of a line Biarritz-Pithiviers (Loiret) – Strasbourg, in regions in which small-scale peasant farming predominated, with growing population pressure on the land. This situation was made worse by the persistent difficulties of market-orientated activities such as vine and silk cultivation, forestry and rural industry in general. To the north and west of this line, in the

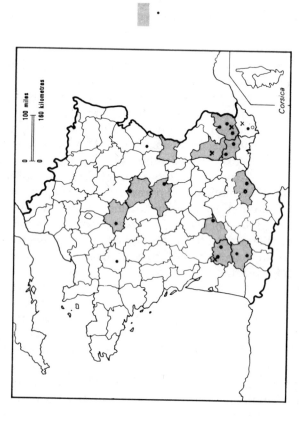

Map VIII   Areas of insurrection in France, December 1851.
Source: Open University, *The Revolutions of 1848* (Unit 2, Milton Keynes, 1976)

departments of western France, the north, north-east and most of the Paris region, there was little disorder. These were in the main either areas of larger-scale commercial farming, in which more advanced industrial development did something to relieve population pressure, and/or zones in which traditional elites supported by the church retained considerable influence. The various risings, localised and uncoordinated as they were, were easily suppressed by the military. They were a last desperate gamble, which nevertheless revealed a degree of commitment on the part of artisans and peasants to the defence of democracy as the means of creating a more egalitarian society and achieving higher living standards – even though the means employed were reminiscent of traditional peasant protest. For conservatives they provided justification for a further intensification of the processes of administrative repression which finally brought to an end the long period of political crisis which had been inaugurated by the February Revolution in 1848[52, 54, 55, 74].

In Germany, as in France, radicals had tended to divide according to the emphasis they placed upon democracy or socialism, and according to the political and social situation in the various states. They were always relatively weak. The democrats failed to win much support from either the middle classes or the workers. The socialists' main achievement was to frighten the predominantly liberal middle classes[119]. Nevertheless in the autumn, winter and spring of 1848–9 they were able to present some opposition to the development of political reaction, and what they regarded as the betrayal of the national cause by the Frankfurt assembly. Democratic congresses organised by a small number of Frankfurt deputies were held in that city in June and in Berlin in October. The latter was overshadowed by disorders on 16 October – involving workers protesting about a reduction in the scale of public works schemes. Eleven of these were killed by middle-class civic guards. Then on 31 October troops dispersed crowds demanding that the Prussian assembly sanction support for revolution in Vienna. The main positive achievement of this Berlin congress was the decision to establish a permanent organisation, the Central March Association (*Zentralmärzverein*), presided over by Julius Fröbel. In the following months 950 local associations adhered to it, with some half-million members, mainly skilled workers, but also members of the lower middle and professional classes. To offset internal divisions on social policy and political tactics, Fröbel sought to take advantage of nationalist sentiment in an effort to persuade state governments to accept the constitutional proposals emerging from Frankfurt. This, inevitably, gave the movement a popular and anti-monarchical character[18, 78, 89, 113].

Further to the left, traditional institutions were clearly significant as a means of radical mobilisation. Thus regional congresses of master artisans were organised between April and July 1848 to prepare programmes for presentation to the Frankfurt parliament. These demanded a return to corporate forms of production, together with restrictions on the development of factories and the reinforcement of tariff protection. They also wanted a progressive income tax, cheap credit, free education, a guaranteed right to work and support for those unable to work. The most likely solution to the problems faced by the owners of small workshops appeared to be help from above, that is the government aid requested in a campaign of petitions to the Assembly. The situation was complicated by the emergence of clear differences of interest between masters and journeymen. The latter were increasingly likely to take strike action, organised their own associations (*Arbeitervereine*) and met separately in a General German Labour Congress between 20 July and 20 September to prepare an independent programme. This included demands for a minimum wage and shorter working day and greater opportunities for journeymen to become master artisans. From September, efforts were made by Stefan Born through an organisation and newspaper entitled *Brotherhood* (*Die Verbrüderung*), based in Leipzig, to appeal to skilled workers in both craft-workshops and factories. By April 1849, branches had been created in some 87 towns with as many as 18,000 members. They combined education and agitation, with mutual aid and cooperative activities. While pressing their various demands, journeymen also made clear their growing anxiety about competition for employment from unskilled labour and the prospect of proletarianisation. They tended to share the middle-class habit of dismissing the mass of unskilled workers as a 'rabble'[76, 89, 112, 118].

The spread of often ephemeral democratic clubs and workers' associations, and the development of the radical press in the winter of 1848–9, was evidence of widespread politicisation and the mobilisation of support for the left. The collapse of governmental authority in March 1848 had provided major new opportunities for expressing grievances and stimulated a much more widespread interest in political activity, particularly amongst those skilled, literate workers who felt most threatened by mechanisation and economic liberalism, and were inspired by a corporate tradition. Middle-class radicals, such as the journalist Friedrich Held or the student Gustave Schlöffel in Berlin appealed to 'the people' in newspapers like *Die Volksfreund* (named after Marat's *Ami du Peuple* of 1792). Nevertheless their essentially democratic political programmes had a limited appeal. Karl Marx, editor of the *Neue Rheinische Zeitung* in Cologne, similarly failed to link political to economic and social reform in a way which might have made politics appear more relevant to workers and peasants. In contrast, in the same city, until his imprisonment, the Utopian socialist Gottschalk enjoyed greater popular support by calling for reductions in the taxes on foodstuffs, and direct financial assistance for artisans and workers. Democrats and radicals were divided over means and ends and were unable to collaborate effectively to devise and communicate an attractive political programme. The left remained geographically fragmented, ideologically divided and faced by increasingly confident conservative and reaction-ary forces. As early as the summer of 1848 it was already evident that mass interest in politics was in steep decline. By November even the establishment of the obviously reactionary Brandenburg–Manteuffel ministry, followed by the proroga-tion of the Prussian Assembly, could only provoke minor protest[112, 114, 124].

On the other hand the disturbed economic situation ensured that social tension remained high. In relatively industrialised Saxony the democratic movement was based on artisans and rural weavers who hoped that manhood suffrage would ensure social reforms and greater security. Tension remained particularly intense in Dresden, Leipzig, Chemnitz and throughout the Vogtland and Erzgebirge. In Franconia, radical politics attracted support especially in the Bamberg area, where particularist opposition to the Bavarian state was strong; in Nuremberg and along the Main valley, amongst groups threatened by commercial capitalism, and by the development of the railways and peasants unwilling to pay compensation to their former seigneurs or to respect the forest laws, all of whom were in close contact with politically more advanced areas in the Rhineland. In Hesse-Darmstadt and Württemberg there was considerable support for the national ideal against princely absolutism. In Baden, in September Struve led an insurrection, which although a pathetic failure, represented a response to the continuing collapse of state authority[89].

It was in these areas that the final acts of resistance to political reaction occurred in May–June 1849. These were characterised by a bitter sense amongst democrats of betrayal by the princes and liberal bourgeoisie following Friedrich Wilhelm's refusal to recognise the Imperial Constitution prepared by the Frankfurt Assembly, and the withdrawal of Prussian delegates. Widespread protest occurred together with uprisings, limited in scale, mainly in the south-west (in Baden, Rhineland-Palatinate, Saxony and Westphalia). These were organised primarily by the popular political societies and were particularly threatening, from the point of view of the authorities, in the Bavarian Palatinate (around Kaiserslautern) and in Baden where they gained support from part at least of the army. In Baden a provincial government was established at Karlsruhe. Typically, however, it was weakened by divisions over tactics between the democrat Brentano and the socialist revolutionary Struve. Other risings occurred in the Prussian Rhineland – with short-lived resistance in the textile centre of Elberfeld involving reserve soldiers of the *Landwehr* – and spread into the industrial areas of Westphalia and Iserlohn. In Dresden, four days of fighting, involving 8000–10,000 insurgents left 250 dead. Prussian troops had to be called in by the Saxon government to restore order. These isolated movements, poorly led and facing regular soldiers, were doomed to failure. The efforts of a rump of the Frankfurt Assembly to maintain an independent existence at Stuttgart, and to call for support from the German people, came to an end on 18 June when their meeting place was closed by troops[86, 92, 98].

To a far greater extent than in Germany, pressures for democratic and social reform in Austria (excluding Bohemia) were limited to the capital city. In Vienna, too, students played a far more important role than elsewhere, joining with the educated middle classes in their enthusiasm for a Greater Germany, into which Austria, in some unspecified fashion, would be merged. In contrast, workers were more concerned with such matters as higher wages, a ten-hour day, limits on the employment of machines, apprentices and women, and assistance for the sick and aged. A degree of unity and direction was provided by the Central Committee of Citizens, Students and the National Guard. The committee championed manhood suffrage, a constituent assembly and work-relief schemes for the unemployed, and in the process increasingly alarmed and alienated political liberals. A reluctant government was gradually forced to make concessions. On 15 May 1848, in response to demonstrations, it conceded the suffrage. On 25 May, when in reaction to decrees closing the university and amalgamating the students' Academic Legion with the National Guard students and workers constructed barricades, the government again chose to capitulate. Continued radical distrust of the emperor's ministers was however, revealed by the establishment of a Security Committee (*Sicherheitausschluss*) led by Dr Fischof. The period from late May to mid-August, during which the government was effectively subordinate to this committee, marked the high point of the radical movement.

Agitation was mounting in the clubs, in the press and on the streets. Criticism of the aristocracy and clergy was becoming more frequent and attitudes towards the person of the emperor increasingly less respectful. This brought to the fore the divisions between democratic middle-class elements and the student leadership on the one hand, with their German nationalist interests, and the workers, on the other with their fundamental concern with greater material security. On 15–16 June and 23 August, workers protesting against low wages and poor working conditions were dispersed by middle-class National Guards. In the second incident, at least six workers

71

were killed. This substantially weakened the democratic alliance. Further polarisation occurred as the economic situation deteriorated throughout August and September and popular misery intensified. Reflecting this, the more radical militants established their own Central Committee of the Democratic Clubs on 3 October. The crisis finally came to a head on 6 October when efforts by crowds to prevent the departure of troops for Hungary led to the pillaging of the arsenal and the murder of the War Minister, General Latour. In these circumstances, and to prevent soldiers coming under the influence of agitators, the army was ordered to withdraw from the city of Vienna. In a situation of extreme confusion, and in the absence of legally constituted authority, the students' Committee and the more radical Central Committee of the Democratic Clubs, acting through a triumvirate of Fischof, Tausenau and Habrowsky, took over. They attempted to prepare the radical elements of the National and Academic Guards, together with workers and deserters from the army to defend the city against the inevitable military reaction. With merely 30,000–40,000 defenders, isolated from the rest of Austria, their only real hope was a Magyar victory over the imperial forces or conciliation by representatives of the Frankfurt Assembly. Neither of these was to materialise, and in the second half of October 70,000 troops under Windischgrätz concentrated around Vienna. From 23 October to 1 November between 2000 and 5000 insurgents were killed as the army regained control[89, 143].

Of the 45 million inhabitants of the German Confederation whose future had been discussed at Frankfurt, some 12 million had belonged to the German-dominated western provinces of the Habsburg Empire. To a large degree the debate on the boundaries of the new German Reich had encapsulated the question of whether it would be dominated by Prussia or Austria. However, concerned as it was to assert its German sense of identity, and with its members frequently affirming feelings of racial superiority over the Slavs, the Assembly was almost bound to reject the inclusion within the German Empire of the vast non-Germanic regions of the Habsburg monarchy, with the exception of areas to which Germans felt they had a 'historic right' such as Bohemia. In this case they were able to muster a whole complex of historical, legal, economic, cultural and racial reasons to justify their claims, and conversely to ignore the ethnic and linguistic claims of the Czechs. Liberals and democrats alike quickly recovered from any initial sympathy with such causes as Polish independence and asserted their support for the German minority in Prussian Poznan, as well as that in Danish ruled Schleswig-Holstein[131, 132]. This all tends to support the emphasis of historians such as Namier, writing in the aftermath of the Second World War, on the illiberal nature of the nationalism of the Frankfurt Assembly[17, 110].

The dream of a Greater Germany was also increasingly challenged by Austrian conservatives and indeed by many liberals. Both were increasingly suspicious of Friedrich Wilhelm of Prussia's ambitions and were unwilling to surrender sovereignty over any part of the Habsburg domains to a new German State. The support of Viennese radicals for the Greater Germany, which they assumed would guarantee political freedom and social reform, only confirmed their worst fears. As Austro-Germans, however, they were also hostile to the claims for independence asserted in the Italian and Hungarian provinces of the empire. In general they seemed incapable of understanding that to non-Germans 'freedom' might mean the end of German dominance. This was also true of the Viennese democrats who welcomed military action against 'the insane or corrupt Slav party of the Czechs [who sought] to turn Austria into a Slav Empire at the expense of the Germans' as the *Volksfreund* put it. These divisions between the nationalities would be effectively exploited by the imperial authorities[124, 143].

In Bohemia the reality was that a small group of militants were insisting upon the distinctiveness of Czech culture and demanding linguistic equality and greater autonomy, while stressing their loyalty to the monarchy. These demands enjoyed support amongst the middle and lower middle classes, amongst businessmen, artisans, and especially intellectuals, groups which combined a Czech sense of identity with resentment at competition from Germans in their business and professional lives, and of the controls imposed by a German bureaucracy.

To a large degree the events of March 1848 in Vienna were imitated in Prague, with the formation by liberal-minded Czechs and Germans of a National Guard to protect freedom and order, and of an Academic Legion and political clubs, and by the publication of newspapers and pamphlets. Most significant of all was a petition organised by the St Václav Committee. Many of its demands were recognised by the hard-pressed government in Vienna in a letter of 8 April. This accepted that the Czech language should enjoy equal status with German in the administration and in education; it promised an administration responsible to a Bohemian Diet at some time in the near future, but it deferred a decision on the proposed union between Bohemia, Moravia and Silesia. Subsequently opposition from German speakers, and the limited national consciousness of many, especially Czechs in the countryside, made it easy for the government to whittle away these concessions. As in the rest of the empire, for the rural populations of Bohemia the vital meaning of 'freedom' was the refusal to meet feudal obligations.

Nevertheless Germans, afraid of losing their dominant position within the empire, had been shocked by such incidents as the rejection of Bohemian representation at Frankfurt by the leading Czech spokesman, the historian Palacký, and by the organisation of a Slav Congress in Prague for 2–12 June. They reacted to Czech demands with the mixture of condescension and contempt typified by Marx and Engel's rejection of the Czech nation's right to a renewed 'historical existence'. Palacký's favoured option was the improvement of the position of the Czechs within a multinational Habsburg Empire, which he maintained could alone offer protection against the alternatives of German or Russian domination. Within the National Committee, established on 13 April to advise the royal governor, and from which German representatives soon withdrew, middle-class Czech liberals like Palacký soon made their fear of a popular movement evident. Their anxieties had been heightened by a wave of strikes, attacks on bakers' premises and on Jewish merchants. They rejected the kind of challenge to the imperial regime which radical proposals for the establishment of a network of committees to organise propaganda and compete with the State bureaucracy might have represented. Nevertheless, and in spite of this conciliatory approach, tension mounted. In March the Prague military command, learning from the experience of Vienna and Milan, had withdrawn from most of the city to the surrounding hillsides: Hradčany, Letná, Petřín and Vyšehrad. However, the return from leave on 20 May of the unpopular General Windischgrätz, a well-connected aristocrat, who like other senior Austrian commanders was prepared to ignore political requests for caution, was followed by intensified military activity, including frequent street patrols, which totally ignored the sensibilities of the city's population. Finally on 12 June, crowds protesting about what appeared to be military preparations to regain control of Prague clashed with troops. Barricades were hastily constructed across the narrow streets of the central Old and New Towns by 1200–1500 insurgents, whose activities were rapidly brought to an end by an artillery bombardment. Of the 43 killed, at least 29 were manual workers. Amongst 63 wounded there were 11 students and one businessman, but again a majority of workers.

This incident provided the authorities with an excuse to ban the National Committee and indefinitely postpone the election of a Bohemian Diet. It left the imperial parliament in Vienna, due to meet on 22 July, as the Czechs' last opportunity. There the most determined opponents of the sort of imperial federation proposed by Palacký were German-speaking radicals who combined their demands for social reform with Great-German chauvinism and often hysterical anti-Slav sentiments. The Czech deputies led by Palacký and most notably František Rieger themselves supported imperial ministers in the hope of receiving concessions in return. Politically they were moderate constitutionalists, afraid of disorder; in relation to economic and social policy they were proponents of *laissez-faire*. Good lawyers, and respectable property-owners, they supported compensation for the loss of feudal privileges, and welcomed the defeat of the Vienna revolt in October. They received hardly anything in return. However, if little was achieved in institutional terms, the experience of 1848 in Bohemia certainly had the effect of stimulating the Czech national consciousness and placing yet

75

another problem on the Habsburg agenda, although it must have seemed quite minor in comparison with the situations prevailing in the Italian and Hungarian portions of the empire[140, 141, 142].

As we have seen, in Italy the news from Vienna in March had encouraged widespread protest in both the Austrian-ruled provinces and the independent states, leading most notably in the latter to the proclamation of constitutions based upon the French model of 1830 with a limited franchise, and in the former to the expulsion of Austrian forces. The apparently impending collapse of Austrian power encouraged Charles Albert, King of Piedmont, Pope Pius IX, the King of Naples and the Grand Duke of Tuscany to commit troops to an effort to expel them finally beyond the Alps. They were inspired by personal ambition, and also responding to complex pressures from liberal elites (aristocratic and middle-class) to work for a united Italy, and also to protect them against republican movements in the newly liberated areas with their talk of manhood suffrage, political liberties and vague ideals of social justice. The largely working-class crowds which had actually defeated the Austrian army were soon transformed into a 'mortal menace' (Cavour). There was also the possibility, as in the 1790s, of intervention (however unlikely this might appear in retrospect given the desire of the French republic to avoid international complications[44]) by a revolutionary French regime which encouraged Italian leaders to insist that Italy would liberate itself (*Italia farà dasè*)[153, 156].

The campaign waged by the Italian states was a fiasco. The mutual suspicions of their leaders were immediately apparent. As early as 29 April Pius IX was led to condemn the war, worried by the twin threats it posed to social order and to the unity of the Catholic world. His prestige suffered considerably from this act, and pressure in Rome for whole-hearted support of the national cause mounted, forcing Pius to take refuge in the Neapolitan port of Gaeta on 24 November, from whence he denounced liberalism and demanded the submission of his subjects. This contributed to a further radicalisation of Roman politics, which resulted in the election of a Constituent Assembly by universal male suffrage, and in the rejection of the Pope's temporal authority and the establishment of a republic in February 1849. In July this was to succumb to a French army sent by Louis-Napoléon to restore the Pope largely as a means of reinforcing Catholic support for his own regime[152]. The alliance against Austria had also been weakened when in May 1848 Ferdinand of Naples had felt confident enough to ignore liberal critics, and to recall his troops from the north for use in internal repression both on the mainland and then in Sicily, where Palermo, which had experienced the first of the European revolutions, was forced to surrender on 15 May 1849.

The main military effort against the Austrians thus came from Piedmont, but in March 1848 Charles Albert's initial hesitancy had allowed the Austrian commander Radetzky to regroup his forces following his expulsion from Milan, to secure reinforcements and recover the initiative, ignoring in the process efforts by his emperor's representatives (anxious about the financial and manpower implications of war in Italy) to negotiate. It also rapidly became evident that support for the nationalist cause – as opposed to anti-Austrian feeling – was limited and frequently conditional. In spite of peasant support for urban insurrection in March and subsequent efforts, particularly in the Veneto by the rural intelligentsia – priests, professional men and merchants – to enrol peasants in local militias, the fundamental unwillingness of the revolutionary governments in Milan and Venice, dominated as they were by property owners, to concede major agrarian reforms, together with requisitioning by the Piedmontese army as it moved into the Lombard plain, alienated much of the rural population, and isolated the revolutionary movements in the cities. For most middle-class republicans – men such as the Venetian leader Manin – the social protest which had followed the revolutions and news of such events as the June 1848 insurrection in Paris only reinforced an already deeply rooted social conservatism[149, 150]. After the failure of regular troops at Custoza in July 1848, the calls of the revolutionary Mazzini for a people's war only added to the fears of most property owners, and attracted little mass support with its vague appeals for revolt 'in the name of God and the people' and lack of precise promises of social reform.

Assisted by the incompetence of the Piedmontese army,

Map IX   Italy in 1848.
Source: Open University, *The Revolutions of 1848* (Unit 2, Milton Keynes, 1982)

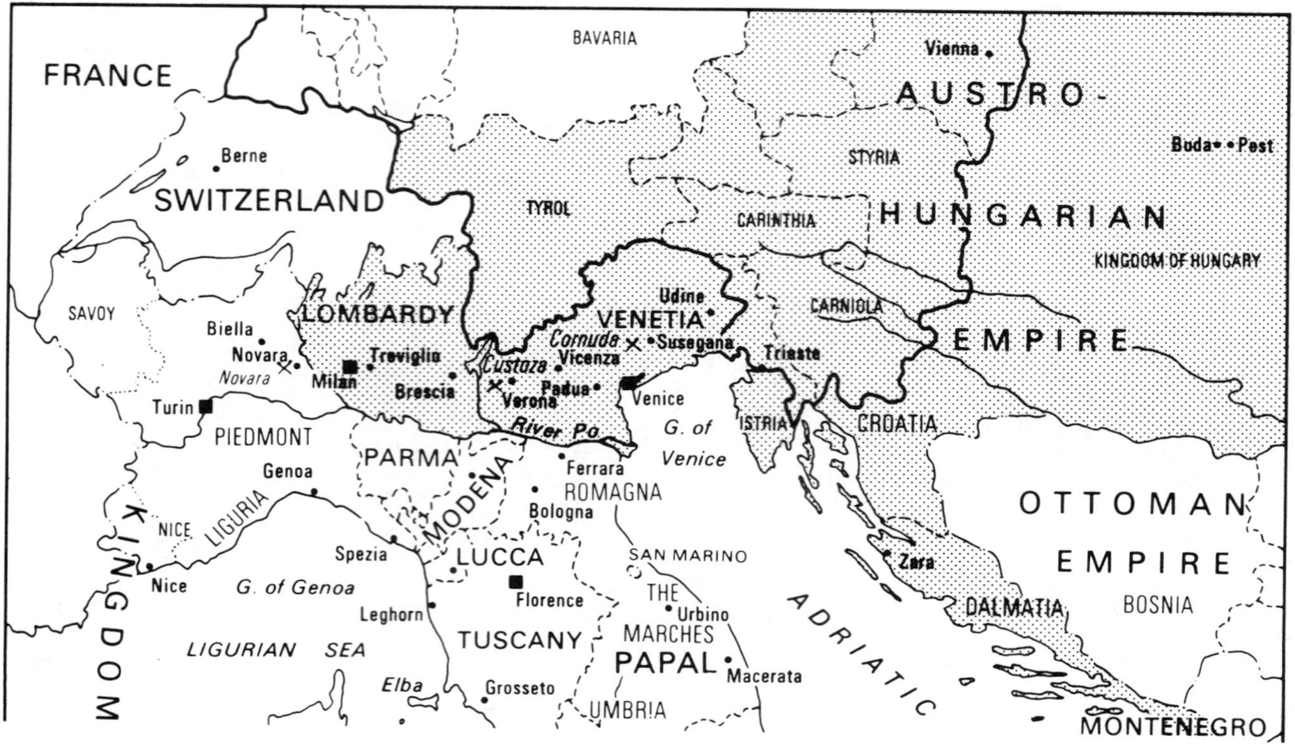

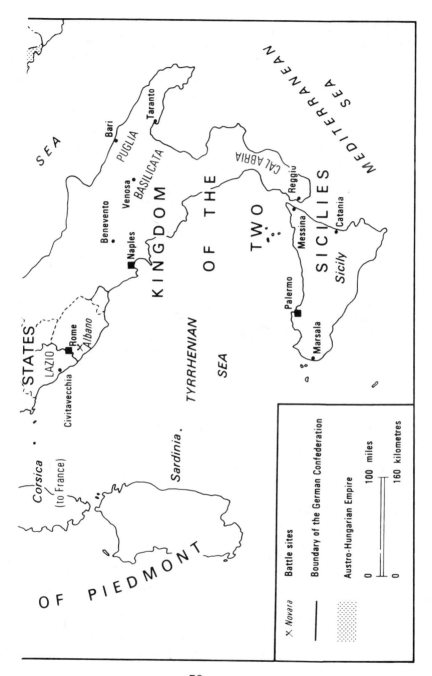

STATES

SEA

Bari

Taranto

PUGLIA

BASILICATA

Venosa

Benevento

Naples

KINGDOM

OF THE

TWO

CALABRIA

Reggio

SICILIES

Messina

Catania

Sicily

Palermo

Marsala

MEDITERRANEAN SEA

Rome
Albano
LAZIO
Civitavecchia

Corsica
(to France)

Sardinia

TYRRHENIAN

SEA

OF   PIEDMONT

X *Novara*   Battle sites

Boundary of the German Confederation

Austro-Hungarian Empire

0   100 miles

0   160 kilometres

Radetzky was able to win a decisive victory at Custoza on 25 July and impose an armistice on 9 August, which made obvious Charles Albert's willingness to abandon Lombardy and Venice to their fates providing the Austrians agreed not to enter Piedmont. In this situation the utterly disillusioned Milanese surrendered without a struggle. Charles Albert's subsequent attempt to restore the prestige of his dynasty by re-entering the war in March 1849 led only to further humiliation at Novara and to his own abdication[145]. The initial impact of this situation was the short-lived radicalisation of some middle-class revolutionary–nationalist groups. In Genoa, supported by artisans and dock workers unhappy at the prospect of Austrian occupation, these demanded the continuation of the war. Similar developments occurred in Florence and, more successfully, at least in the short term, in Rome under the leadership of Mazzini and Garibaldi. More significantly, however, this final Piedmontese defeat eliminated the main obstacle to the restoration of Austrian predominance and to a wave of repressive measures, replicated in the Papal states, and particularly in the Kingdom of Naples where 15,000 suspected supporters of opposition to the monarchy were arrested. Only Venice, protected by its lagoons, held out. It was subjected to an ever more effective Austrian blockade and finally forced to capitulate on 22 August 1849 as food supplies ran out and social tension and middle-class fear of social revolt grew. On 27 August imperial troops, significantly led by a Hungarian regiment, re-entered the city[150].

The collapse of the central government in Vienna had given an opportunity to those Hungarians such as Széchenyi and Kossuth – modernisers, anxious to create a liberal, industrial society – who had previously agitated for greater autonomy within the empire, as well as for vague, limited measures of land reform as a means of winning mass support[134]. The April Laws of 1848, presented by the Hungarian Diet to the emperor, provided for equality before the law, the abolition of peasant labour service and of tithes – with compensation provided – and of noble tax privileges, and for a liberal political constitution by establishing a property-based franchise which gave the vote to about a quarter of adult males. One

80

consequence was to ensure the continued hegemony of the relatively large noble class in the new house of representatives elected in June, where 74 per cent of the deputies were nobles (titled or untitled), as well as in the County administration. Another consequence was the establishment of a considerable degree of independence for Hungary.

With the empire apparently on the verge of collapse, and most of the army tied down in Italy, the authorities in Vienna believed that they had little alternative but to accept these proposals[145]. The viceroy, the emperor's representative, the Archduke Stephen, appointed Battyány, one of the country's wealthiest landowners, as prime minister in Hungary. Battyány in turn presented to the Diet a list of ministers composed entirely of representatives of the landowning nobility. These were united in their determination to resist threats to this newly established Hungarian autonomy from Austria as well as to their predominance within the lands of the crown of Hungary. This was likely to come from ethnic minorities anxious to preserve their own 'freedoms', from the small numbers of political radicals and urban workers, anxious to promote further social and political reform, or more threateningly from peasants dissatisfied with rights of access to common land and forests, and in some regions already engaging in attacks on landlords and Jewish merchants. The kind of far-reaching land reform which might have attracted committed peasant support to the new regime was unthinkable to noble landowners.

The concessions made by Vienna facilitated the immediate preservation of the personal union of the Austrian and Hungarian crowns. However, the agreements reached on the shared responsibility for finance, foreign policy and the army remained dangerously ambiguous. As the military situation of the imperial government improved it would become apparent to Hungarian leaders that the price of continued autonomy would be more radical measures of self-defence. At this stage too, many of the wealthier aristocrats, with their close connections with the imperial court, would abandon the national cause. Moreover greater Hungarian assertiveness also had the adverse effect of stimulating resistance by non-Magyar groups and particularly the Croatians and Transylvan-

81

ian Romanians to Magyar efforts to impose linguistic and administrative uniformity. These would respond positively to imperial hints of greater autonomy and the promise to abolish feudalism. Mounting tension between ethnic groups soon degenerated into a vicious cycle of atrocity and counter-atrocity[137, 139, 146].

A struggle with the imperial government was probably inevitable once it felt powerful enough to take a military initiative. The German-Austrian-dominated imperial bureaucracy certainly felt that the Hungarian reformers had demanded greater autonomy than was compatible with the survival of the empire. From mid-June 1848 resistance to Magyar pretensions led by Jelačić and other Croat nobles was encouraged. Matters rapidly came to a head. In July Kossuth asked the Diet to refuse to send any more Hungarian troops to Italy, and to approve the recruitment of an army to defend Hungary. On 31 August the imperial government ordered the abolition of separate Hungarian finance and war ministries. On 11 September an attempt by the viceroy to seize Buda-Pest was frustrated and on 21 September the Hungarian parliament elected a National Defence Committee, which became the effective government of the country under Kossuth's leadership. Further fuel was added to the flames on 28 September when an imperial commissioner, Count Lemberg, was assassinated in Pest, an incident followed by imperial decrees dissolving the Hungarian parliament, invalidating its resolutions, and establishing martial law. In this situation, and in marked contrast with other liberal parliaments in 1848, that which represented the Magyar social elites would feel threatened primarily by external forces rather than internal revolution.

The Hungarian army, composed of former imperial (c. 50,000 men) and newly raised regiments (c. 120,000 by June 1849) initially experienced some success in resisting Jelačić's incursions, and on 30 October came within a few miles of Vienna, but its failure then to provide support for the insurgents in the city led to the final crushing of the Viennese revolution two days later. Together with the successes of the imperial army in Italy, this meant that it was only a matter of time before substantial military forces would be concentrated against the Hungarians. As a result in December the Hungarian government and parliament were forced to abandon Buda and trek by carriage and cart to Debrecen, a large village on the Great Plain. There, growing discouragement inspired by defeat and the practical difficulties of raising men and money, led to increased political factionalism. Support for peace negotiations grew but was thwarted by imperial demands for unconditional surrender. Moreover, all did not appear to be lost. During April 1849 the Austrians were again driven out of most of the country, a reverse which persuaded the panicky Austrian commanders to recommend the humiliating acceptance of Russian offers of military assistance. The Tsar had partially mobilised his forces on news of the February Revolution in Paris, so they were ready to move shortly after receipt of the new Austrian Emperor Franz Joseph's public appeal for aid in 'the holy struggle against anarchy'. In retrospect this intervention was hardly necessary, given the growing exhaustion of the Hungarian army.

In this situation Kossuth was unable to combat a growing belief that the war was lost, and indeed between August and October the Hungarian armies were defeated or forced to surrender. This finally brought to an end the Revolutions of 1848. The human cost had been high. An estimated 50,000 Hungarians are believed to have been killed, and a similar number of Austrians. Following the surrender about 120 rebels were executed, and an unknown number found with arms in hand were summarily killed. Over 150 others were sentenced to between ten and twenty years imprisonment. In addition, while only 500 Russians died in battle, over 11,000 died of cholera[135, 139].

In their various ways the Revolutions had seemed to bring closer the prospect of more egalitarian societies, and in the east of greater autonomy for some ethnic groups. There had been little agreement however, amongst the supporters of political and social reform on the positive measures to be taken. Liberals, democrats, radicals and socialists had engaged in bitter disputes. This had made it difficult to mobilise and sustain mass support, particularly amongst the rural population. Amongst urban workers the sense of a common interest in social reform, of class identity, had certainly been enhanced, but even so, loyalties to craft and locality remained far stronger. The most significant effect of those measures of social reform which were introduced, or even appeared in prospect, was to arouse substantial and growing opposition, not only from the old elites but also from large sections of the propertied classes, easily satisfied by a modicum of constitutional change and frightened by widespread disorder and the threat of social revolution. The old regimes of central and eastern Europe moreover enjoyed a considerable degree of success in retaining peasant support by means of the final abolition of feudalism. This together with the obvious divisions and consequent weakness of the political left had eased the path for the development of counter-revolution.

5   Counter-revolution

With the benefit of hindsight it is easy to see that a conservative reaction against revolutionary change was inevitable, and that it enjoyed every prospect of success. In the first place, in Austria and Prussia, while leading to the appointment of new ministers, revolution had left existing monarchs with considerable executive power, involving in each case control over the bureaucracy and army. Friedrich Wilhelm IV and, on his accession in December, Franz Joseph were committed to eventual reaction, and encouraged in this by their aristocratic advisers. In Prussia men such as the adjutant-general, Leopold von Gerlach, and Junker nobles such as Kleist-Retzau, von Below or the young Bismarck, were all ferociously anti-liberal, inspired by a pietistic religious faith and a soldier's sense of loyalty[98]. Even in France much of the old bureaucracy and especially the army officer corps had remained in place. The June insurrection in Paris had then frightened the democratically elected Constituent Assembly into appointing the conservative republican General Cavaignac as head of government, to be followed in December by the election of the Bonapartist pretender, Louis-Napoléon, as President of the Republic[49, 67].

The old social elites had soon recovered from the demoralisation they initially experienced with the apparent collapse of the existing institutions of government. They possessed the considerable advantage of a sense of social and cultural superiority, a growing appreciation of the need for unity when faced with a clear threat to their status, the benefit of entrenched positions in the civil service and army, and experience of politics. To this might be added control of considerable organisational resources and the ability to exercise influence through their roles as landowners, employers and in local government[50, 66, 124]. In the special circumstances of 1848 a major effort seemed to be required to restore their power. In Prussia the disastrous results of the May 1848 elections had convinced most conservatives of this and the summer of 1848 saw the creation of monarchist associations throughout the countryside, together with a coordinating 'Association for the Protection of Property and the Advancement of the Welfare of all Classes', the so-called 'Junker Parliament' which met in Berlin in August. Another basis for coordinated action was provided by a new newspaper, the *Kreuzzeitung* inspired by Gerlach, Bismark and Wagener, with its condemnation of manhood suffrage, its demand instead for the representation of 'interests', its Prussian particularism, Protestant pietism and anti-semitism. A mixture of concessions to the peasants, and an exaggerated representation of the threat posed by the left to property, religion, the family and nation, all helped to win mass support. In the towns 'Prussian Unions' (*Preussenverein*) called upon the lower middle classes and workers to show loyalty to their king, and encouraged attacks on the persons and property of leading liberals and democrats[91].

Similarly in German Austria, by September at the latest, concessions together with the exercise of 'influence' had rendered the mass of the rural population indifferent or positively hostile to the revolution, effectively isolating the Viennese radicals[143]. In contrast with these efforts, the attempts by the left to win peasant support were generally ill-conceived. In France, it was only after the revolutionary movement in Paris had been crushed, and in the aftermath of Bonaparte's stunning election victory in December 1848[70] that a concerted radical effort to win over the predominantly small-town and rural electorate took place[34, 51]. Everywhere, and in spite of tensions between the Protestant Prussian state and its Roman Catholics, the churches served as bastions of conservatism, while attempting to manipulate the political situation in their own interests. In Germany this involved the encouragement of mass organisations such as the Catholic *Piusverein*. Everywhere the clergy sought increased influence over education. The anti-clericalism of much of the left probably made this inevitable, just as the churches' conservatism in 1848 reinforced anti-clerical feelings[89].

The influence of the established elites was further strengthened by the growing desire in all social groups for the peace and social order which seemed to be the prerequisite for economic recovery. The middle classes in particular were frightened by radical propaganda and the apparent threat to their property. Their worst fears seemed confirmed by news of the June insurrection in Paris. In France many moderate republicans, and elsewhere constitutional liberals – interested essentially in acquiring rights of political participation for themselves by means of limited constitutional reform – were soon disillusioned by the course of events. In Vienna the liberal poet Grillparzer published a poem on 8 June 1848 addressed 'To Field Marshal Radetzky' appealing to him, 'Now strike home'. Increasingly the main threat to the rule of law appeared to come from those denounced in the conservative press as agents of foreign powers, corrupters of youth, anarchists and communists, who were leading astray the undisciplined masses, rather than from authoritarian government. Social and ethnic divisions rapidly destroyed the initial enthusiasm for reform and any sense of unity amongst its proponents. A process of political polarisation occurred with a large majority of the original supporters of limited reforms opting for a conservative rather than a radical outcome to the post-revolutionary crisis[55, 119].

Of particular significance in determing the results of the ensuing conflict was the continuing ability of old elites to control state bureaucracies and armies. The feeble efforts of liberal ministers and elected assemblies to gain control over the military were resisted. Nowhere did more than mild purges of the officer corps occur. While civilian National Guards were created or expanded the motives of those enrolled varied – between the desire of some radicals to create an alternative centre of power to the army, and the far more common middle-class objective of assisting in the maintenance of public order. Anyway, neither they nor the insurgents were a match for disciplined regular troops given clear objectives. In the last resort soldiers usually employed violence more effectively and proved so on the streets of Paris, Prague, Milan, Vienna, Berlin, Dresden and many other places. To some extent the military constituted an independent power base preparing for counter-revolution. Its officer corps, largely made up of nobles (with the partial exception of the French) was inspired by an institutionalised ideal of loyalty to the state, but interpreted in a fashion which corresponded to the interests of their class of origin and its commitment to the defence of 'Christian civilisation' and the established social order[37]. The rank and file, subject to military discipline, separated from their communities of origin and isolated from political debate, were generally determined to remain loyal to their comrades and to reject the appeals of political agitators. Faced by hostile crowds, they normally obeyed the orders of their military superiors[58].

This was particularly evident in Austria, where the aristo-cratic army commanders Windischgrätz, Schwarzenberg, Radetzky and Jelačić played such an important role in the restoration of imperial authority in Vienna and over the diverse provinces of the empire. In spite of a crisis of discipline in many units in the immediate aftermath of the March 1848 Revolution, and widespread desertions, particularly from Italian and Hungarian regiments stationed in their home countries, the continued loyalty of most military units to the empire attested to the professional competence of their commanders, and more especially to the integrating effects of the incorporation of recruits within military units and of their isolation from civilians[136, 145]. For similar reasons, throughout Europe massed troops could be deployed in a show of force to overawe potential opponents and to regain control by brute force in insurgent areas. In Italy and Hungary large military formations were also employed against other regular forces, with the imperial forces emerging victorious in these circumstances to a large extent because of the even greater deficiencies in tactical leadership and control displayed by their enemies. In Germany and France in contrast they were used mainly against civilian insurgents in order to regain control over urban centres, and in mobile columns against rural insurgents in south-west Germany in 1849, and in south-east France in December 1851[52].

It was on the basis of this combination of an increasingly conservative political consensus and the existence of military support that a range of counter-revolutionary measures could be developed successfully. Conservative elites could employ a complex of informal means to influence and, if necessary, coerce tradesmen, workers and peasants. Propaganda presented the 'reds' as plotting to destroy society in an orgy of looting and murder. Electoral systems were manipulated, suspect local officials purged, newspapers and meeting places closed, and radicals intimidated. The result in many areas was effectively to demobilise radical political movements and opposition to political reaction. In France, the June insurrection was succeeded by a long period of growing repression. Immediately afterwards the conservative republican government, headed by General Cavaignac, introduced measures severely restricting the activities of political clubs (28 July 1848) and the press (9–11 August). These were regarded as too moderate by most conservatives. On 4 November the Constituent Assembly approved a constitution which avoided any commitment to the reforming measures discussed before the June insurrection. The republic they now sought to create was to be a liberal democracy entirely bereft of welfare institutions. The retention of manhood suffrage, however, contributed to the survival of a radical (*démocrate-socialiste*) movement, as well as to high levels of conservative anxiety. Fortunately for them, the constitution additionally provided for the election of a president, who was, as the guardian of order, to be provided with wide executive powers[49].

As a result, a further step in the direction of reaction was taken on 10 December 1848 with the election to this office of Louis-Napoléon Bonaparte, the nephew of the great emperor. His major asset was undoubtedly the name. This associated him with a cult of the emperor kept alive by an outpouring of books, pamphlets and lithographs and with the legend of a more prosperous, happy and glorious epoch which contrasted sharply with the economic depression and social strife which seemed to have accompanied the republic. The misery of interminable war seems to have been largely forgotten. The initial opposition to the candidature of Bonaparte from most conservative leaders and newspapers turned into an opportunistic and qualified adhesion as it became evident that he was likely to attract substantial electoral support, often, and alarmingly, in spite of the advice given to voters by their social superiors. Unable amongst themselves to agree on a candidate likely to defeat him, members of the conservative political elite were increasingly drawn into support for Louis-Napoléon. He seemed to be weak; a clown they could manipulate. He appeared to be committed to restoring social order. At the very least his election would prevent consolidation of the republic. The role of influential political figures previously associated with the July Monarchy such as Molé, Barrot, Marshal Bugeaud and especially Thiers, was crucial. Cavaignac, the only real alternative, was essentially the candidate of the moderate republicans. Although he did attract some conservative support, as the man who had proved himself in repressing the June insurrection, for most monarchist notables he was still too much of a republican. He was also rejected by many radical republicans as the 'butcher of June'. Many republicans, believing that the great emperor had continued the work of the revolution, also failed to see that a vote for his nephew was incompatible with their republican principles. This was the great strength of the Bonapartist legend. It allowed Louis-Napoléon to appear as 'all things to all men', as a figure above existing party struggles. His victory in December was overwhelming[36, 67].

The process of counter-revolution in France, which began with the repression of the June insurrection, culminated in the coup-d'état organised by Bonaparte in December 1851. This was an expression of his personal ambitions but also represented the failure of a repressive conservative government to eliminate entirely radical organisation and propaganda – much of which had simply been driven underground – and a growing conviction that in spite of the renewed restriction of the franchise, a radical republican electoral victory remained possible in 1852. For most conservatives, authoritarian government seemed preferable and this feeling was reinforced by the scale of opposition to the coup-d'état. In the major cities – overawed by obvious military preparedness – this was limited, but unexpected resistance occurred in rural areas of central and south-eastern France involving artisans and peasants, led usually by middle-class professional men. As we have seen, these essentially localised insurrections were easily repressed by the army. They were followed by the final settling of accounts with the left which conservatives had desired so ardently. Republican leaders were arrested, driven into exile, or frightened into inactivity. The very act of resistance seemed to justify the coup, which could now be presented as a preventive action. In the plebiscite which followed, the electorate was asked to approve the President's actions and the extension of his authority. The choice, it was claimed, was between *la civilisation et le barbarie, la société et le chaos*. 7,500,000 voted 'yes', 640,000 'no', and 1,500,000 abstained, with opposition concentrated in the major cities. In spite of the repressive atmosphere there is little doubt that most Frenchmen approved of the coup and looked forward to the re-establishment of the empire[52, 74].

This combination of military power and a return to authoritarian government was evident in all those areas which had experienced revolution. It could be seen in the appointment by monarchs of ministers who quite clearly did not enjoy the confidence of parliaments. In Austria the nomination by the victorious Windischgrätz of his brother-in-law, Prince Felix Schwarzenberg, as Chancellor in November 1848 brought to the forefront a man dedicated to the modernisation, centralisation and Germanisation of the monarchy, but realistic enough to recognise that some concessions still needed to be made to the middle-class aspiration to participate in political debate, as well as to nationalist sentiment. This was followed in December by the announcement of the Emperor Ferdinand's abdication in favour of the youthful Franz Joseph, a change which made the disavowal of earlier concessions all the easier because the new emperor had not sworn to uphold them. Symbolically he styled himself 'Emperor by the Grace of God', a form which had been abandoned in March by his predecessor.

The Austrian parliament, exiled to the little Moravian town of Kremsier, continued to discuss a new imperial constitution. This would include such provisions as the abolition of titles of nobility, a reduction in the status of the church, greater provincial autonomy as a concession to the various nationalities, and the restriction of the emperor's power to a suspensive veto, all utterly unacceptable to Franz Joseph. The parliament was increasingly ignored by ministers. Its final dissolution on 7 March 1849, by troops, was hardly unexpected. On the same day Franz Joseph imposed a new constitution, together with a bill of rights which maintained the monarch's absolute right of veto over all legislation, suppressed ministerial responsibility to parliament, restricted the franchise, reduced Hungarian autonomy and strengthened the powers of the central administration. This reactionary movement was reinforced by the work of the military courts in the Italian provinces, and in Hungary where public floggings and hangings were supposed to safeguard Austrian rule, but can have done little to endear the regime to its reluctant subjects. Further reaction would occur in the 1850s, as the young emperor asserted himself in order to eliminate representative institutions (patent of 31 December 1851) and to increase the influence of the Roman Catholic church, particularly in education (1853 Concordat)[135, 143, 145].

In Prussia, September 1848 saw moves by Friedrich Wilhelm to restore his authority, with the appointment of Wrangel as military commander in Berlin, the return of troops to the capital, and the replacement of the liberal Hansemann ministry by a non-parliamentary government briefly headed by General Pfuel, fresh from restoring order in Posen. In his turn he was replaced in mid-October by Manteuffel and General Count Brandenburg, the illegitimate son of Friedrich Wilhelm II, both of whom were determined to restore order and were encouraged by the crushing of the Viennese revolution. One of the first acts of this government was to order the transfer of the Prussian parliament to the small provincial town of Brandenburg, supposedly as a means of protecting it from popular pressure. Those deputies who attempted to meet in Berlin were dispersed by troops. Protest demonstrations in the provinces and calls for a tax strike had little impact. Most middle-class liberals were desperately anxious to avoid acts which might encourage mass revolt. On 5 December the assembly was dissolved finally, and a constitution promulgated by royal decree. It was still felt necessary to make significant concessions to the liberal viewpoint on such matters as equality before the law, rights of association, budgetary control by parliament, and enfranchisement of independent citizens, but not on the crucial question of crown prerogatives.

In spite of the progress made by the counter-revolution, the elections held in January 1849 secured only a small conservative majority, and were followed by the introduction of a new electoral law on 30 May 1849, establishing a three-class system in which voters were placed according to the level of tax they paid in one of three electoral colleges (containing respectively 5, 12 and 83 per cent of the electorate), each electing an equal number of deputies – a system designed to ensure the predominance of wealthy conservatives (land-owners in the eastern, and the upper middle classes in the western provinces of the kingdom). This was justified as allowing to the 'several classes of the people an influence proportionate to their actual importance in the life of the State'[95, 98]. The elections which followed in June resulted, inevitably, in a conservative triumph, with a lower chamber composed of large landowners (22.5 per cent), *grands bourgeois* (5 per cent) and high officials (49.7 per cent). Not surprisingly it welcomed the constitutional revisions published on 31 January 1850, which restored the king's absolute right of veto over legislation, granted extensive authority to rule by decree, and eliminated the right of parliament to refuse to grant taxation. This process by which the authority of the King of Prussia was restored had important consequences for the other German states, freeing the Prussian army for use against democrats in Saxony, the Palatinate and Baden. Only in the last of these was serious resistance offered by some 45,000 men, including 20,000 trained soldiers, throughout June and early July 1849[89]. Thus throughout Continental Europe the nature of politics had once again been transformed, as the powers of elected assemblies were massively reduced, and administrative and military repression directed at those who sought to protest.

6 Conclusions

The processes of political response within a changing social environment were extremely complex. Diverse communities, and social and cultural groups developed what they assumed to be appropriate political styles. From the historian's point of view it would be a gross over-simplification to read the history of 1848 in terms simply of class conflict, although this was rarely absent. Thus in the early stages of the various revolutions while members of the middle classes demanded political representation, workers and peasants sought, above all else, economic security. Subsequently many members of all of these groups came to desire a return to 'normal' in the hope that order would restore prosperity. This strengthened the capacity for reaction of established elites. At the same time other members of these groups continued to oppose political reaction until the costs of resistance became too high. Nationalism, although far less intense than it would become, was another sentiment cutting across social divisions. Clearly then it is not possible to assume that the members of a social group shared the same political objectives, but neither is it sensible to conclude that political activity can be reduced to a random collection of individual states of mind.

The most obvious short-term result of political reaction was the growth of repression. Legislation restricting the freedoms of speech and rights of association and publication was enforced and strengthened. Martial law was established where the authorities were concerned that the surviving legal rights of those thought guilty of sedition might obstruct the process of depoliticisation. In the longer term, policing networks were strengthened and enlarged civil police forces created to allow more constant and efficient supervision of potential trouble-makers. This had the added advantage of limiting the number of occasions on which demonstrators and the military clashed.

95

These incidents, given military tactics and weaponry, had frequently resulted in a heightening of the levels of violence, and could have such untoward consequences as the February Revolution. In the last resort, however, military power remained available, to be deployed in order to increase substantially the costs of protest. Moreover, improved communications by rail and telegraph increasingly allowed the more rapid concentration of troops.

An additional long-term strategy was to promote the more effective integration of potentially discontented social groups into changing political systems. Coercion was combined with ideological manipulation designed to increase regime legitimacy. 1848 had seen the breakdown of the administrative and coercive capacity of a number of states due to a widespread loss of confidence in those who possessed political power. This initial collapse had been followed by the creation of a new conservative consensus based upon fear of revolution. In order to preserve this, established elites were to reveal a willingness to recognise limited political rights while retaining control over bureaucratic and military institutions. In social systems as diverse as those of France, the German States, and Austria–Hungary an extended suffrage, together with representative institutions, was retained, but with severe constraints placed upon the rights of participants. The objective remained political demobilisation. Even so, this was tacit acceptance that the clock could not be turned back all the way. The political awareness of large numbers of people had been stimulated. Whatever their allegiances, more people had been persuaded of the relevance of politics to their daily lives. Doubtless most of them soon lapsed into apathy, but many continued to take at least an episodic interest in affairs outside their own communities. The development of communications, of education and growing governmental interference within communities would serve to reinforce these trends.

This short, but intense, period of crisis thus had a long-term impact upon attitudes. On the one hand fear of social revolution and of the destabilising potential of nationalism was intensified, and on the other older notions of moral economy and natural justice were reinforced by the increasing use of formal political ideology whose basic concepts and slogans were spread to even the remotest communities by middle-class intermediaries. In between, while retaining a preference for parliamentary institutions and the rule of law, liberals and moderate republicans more obviously identified themselves with the need to preserve social order. This middle-class conservatism was to be a crucial factor reinforcing political stability in the following years.

Much has been written about the uniqueness of German history (the *Sonderweg*) in terms of the failure of the middle classes in 1848 to press for the establishment of a liberal state. Marx castigated the German *bourgeoisie* for its 'treachery against the people' and willingness to 'compromise with the crowned representative of the old society' and for its inability to defend its supposed *real* interests and carry through the sort of *bourgeois* revolution that he assumed had occurred in Britain and France. This was due to the fear created by the revolutionary threat to private property and existing social relationships which was to be such a potent factor in allowing the monarchy, together with the pre-industrial elite, to retain its political predominance. More recently this illiberalism of the German middle classes has frequently been linked to the conditions which subsequently led both to the outbreak of war in 1914 and to the Nazi seizure of power. This model however ignores the survival and capacity for adaptation of pre-industrial elites even in those countries with which comparisons have been drawn. Fear of social revolution amongst the possessing classes was an European-wide phenomenon, as was their tendency to blame discontent amongst the lower orders upon drunkenness, ignorance and greed and to deny the legitimacy of a desire for greater material security in a more egalitarian society. Throughout Europe both conservatives and liberals appealed to the military to protect Christian civilisation against 'wild beasts' intent upon 'pillage, rape and arson' as the *Revue des Deux Mondes* described the June insurgents in Paris. This sort of perception ensured the development amongst the property-owning classes of support for strong government and the combination of administrative measures with less formal social pressures which ensured the arrest or exile of radicals, the criminalisation of their activities, and the ostracism which drove them out of public life.

97

Authoritarian government did much to restore business confidence, and contributed to the economic growth evident from the 1850s. In a generally favourable international situation, investment in improved communications and urban renewal stimulated trade and production in both towns and countryside. Rising prosperity, from which most people benefited, helped to reconcile them to illiberal political regimes. In Germany the migration of about a million people during the 1850s also helped to relieve population pressure on resources. In much of central and eastern Europe although the survival of large estates, and the sub-division of their own property combined to ensure that most of the rural population continued to live in close dependence upon old elites, at least the abolition of serfdom had eased the pressure upon them and even – within strict limits – created a greater sense of independence. Governments also made major efforts to reinforce social and political stability through education. Primary instruction for the masses was viewed, in the French education law of 1850 (*loi Falloux*) and in the similar Prussian and Austrian acceptance of an enlarged role in the instruction of the young for the established churches, as a means of socialisation. It was assumed that it would ensure the internalisation of conservative norms and values, and that together with the process of economic integration it would stimulate a greater sense of national unity.

All this added up to a restoration of the authority of the state which made the prospect of revolution increasingly less likely. These measures served to limit the bounds of the political imagination. Practical aspirations were restricted to gradual change within existing social and political systems. The course of events also suggests that revolution in nineteenth-century Europe was in large part the product of a chronologically limited historical period – of transition towards industrialisation – during which accelerating economic and social change affected societies which were still suffering from the older strains of population pressure upon resources and intermittent dearth. It was the political disputes created by these diverse strains which served to destabilise existing regimes.

Subsequently, due to a combination of factors, revolutions

were less likely to occur. These included more effective repression, a greater conservatism on the part of middle classes now aware of the dangers of revolution, and the more successful integration of the masses into the wider society by means of education and, at least in the west, the gradual institutionalisation of protest through trade unions and legalised political activity. These measures combined with greater prosperity and security (in spite of widespread poverty) to effect the isolation of revolutionary minorities – save (as the Franco–Prussian and First World War would reveal) in the exceptional circumstances of war. Then once again widespread misery, the disintegration of the armed forces, and a generalised loss of confidence in governments, which had demonstrably failed, would create a potentially revolutionary situation. Yet to an important degree the wars of the second part of the century were themselves a legacy of 1848. The 'Year of Revolutions' had resulted in a substantial growth in tension between the various ethnic groups inhabiting central and eastern Europe, in increased hostility towards the Austrians in Italy, and greater Austro–Prussian rivalry for influence in Germany. Moreover, political decisions would continue to be taken by small groups, informed largely by their perception of the interests of the narrow social elites to which they belonged, and in a fashion which only incidentally took into account the concerns of the masses. Only gradually, and to a limited extent, as it became evident that opposition groups were themselves not likely to support revolution, did governments begin to make more substantial concessions to political reform, and did repression become more selective.

In so many respects, over large areas of the Continent, the crisis beginning with the poor harvests of 1845–6 which were a major contributory factor to the outbreak of revolution in 1848, and continuing until 1848–51, marked the end of the *ancien régime*. Subsequently the interrelated processes of industrialisation, urbanisation and the commercialisation of agriculture, underway since at least the early eighteenth century, would accelerate and produce major changes in social structures. 1848 – just like 1789 – was then the product of a transition society and of tensions which had grown as part of the process of economic change. These had increased dissatisfaction with political systems which were patently unrepresentative, and what was probably even worse, whose leading figures, because of the situation of crisis, appeared uncaring and incompetent. The subsequent failure of the revolutionaries, together with the continued capacity for reaction of the old elites, permitted a successful conservative recovery. It provided a breathing space during which established elites could develop a more flexible long-term strategy for survival which combined concessions designed to preserve the consensus established amongst men of property by their shared fear of social revolution, with social engineering employing in particular education as the primary means for spreading conservative social values amongst the masses. Although it was increasingly seen as a last resort, and used more sparingly in the years before 1914, the machinery of state repression was also kept well oiled. In these respects the particular combination of institutions and policies which characterise the modern state owes much to the experience of 1848 and to the conservative reaction which followed.

Select Bibliography

Place of publication is London unless otherwise stated.

General Books

[1] E. N. and P. R. Anderson, *Political Institutions and Social Change in Continental Europe in the Nineteenth Century* (1967). A mine of information with useful analysis.

[2] J. Blum, *The End of the Old Order in Rural Europe* (1978). Useful, but with a somewhat dated legalistic approach.

[3] J. Breuilly, *Nationalism and the State* (Manchester, 1982). Stimulating comparative study.

[4] C. Calhoun, 'Industrialisation and Social Radicalism', *Theory and Society* 12 (1983).

[5] K. Chorley, *Armies and the Art of Revolution* (1943). Remains a useful analytical study.

[6] C. H. Church, *Europe in 1830: Revolution and Political Change* (1983). Dependable general survey.

[7] J. R. Gillis, 'Political Decay and the European Revolution, 1789–1848', *World Politics*, XXII (1970).

[8] J. Godechot, *Les Révolutions de 1848* (Paris, 1971).

[9] R. J. Goldstein, *Political Repression in Nineteenth Century Europe* (1983). Informative, but not analytical enough.

[10] T. H. Greene, *Comparative Revolutionary Movements* (1974). Like others of its kind: an aid to the formulation of questions.

[11] R. Grew (ed.) *Crises of Political Development in Europe and the United States* (1978).

[12] P. Jones, *The 1848 Revolutions* (1981). Includes a selection of documents.

[13] E. Kamenka and F. B. Smith (eds), *Intellectuals and Revolution. Socialism and the Experience of 1848* (1979).

[14] E. Labrousse, 'Comment naissent les révolutions. 1848–1830–1789', *Actes du congrès historique du centenaire de la révolution* (Paris, 1948) A classic, influential in its time.

[15] R. Lougee, *Mid Century Revolution, 1848. Society and Politics in France and Germany* (1972).

[16] K. Marx and F. Engels, *The Revolutions of 1848*, ed. D. Fernbach (1973).

[17] L. Namier, *1848. The Revolution of the Intellectuals* (1946). Another classic, but more obviously dated.

[18] Open University, *The Revolutions of 1848* (16 units) (Milton Keynes,

1976). Mixed in quality, but overall quite an achievement – accompanied by radio and television programmes.

[19] C.-H. Pouthas *et al.*, *Démocratie, Réaction, Capitalisme, 1848–1860* (Paris, 1983).

[20] J. Sigmann, *1848* (1973).

[21] A. Sked (ed.), *Europe's Balance of Power, 1815–1848* (1979). Useful for the diplomatic background.

[22] G. Stedman Jones, 'The Mid-Century Crisis and the 1848 Revolutions', *Theory and Society*, 12 (1983).

[23] P. N. Stearns, *The Revolutions of 1848* (1974).

[24] S. Taylor, *Social Science and Revolution* (1984).

[25] C. Tilly and J. Rule, *Measuring Political Upheaval* (Princeton, N.J., 1965).

[26] C., L. and R. Tilly, *The Rebellious Century* (1975).

[27] C. Tilly, *From Mobilization to Revolution* (1978). Always suggestive, if excessively schematic.

[28] M. Traugott, 'The Mid-Nineteenth Century Crisis in England and France' *Theory and Society*, 12 (1983).

[29] E. Zimmermann, *Political Violence, Crises, and Revolution* (1983).

France

[30] M. Agulhon, *The Republic in the Village. The People of the Var from the French Revolution to the Second Republic* (1982). A classic – linking local politics to national movements.

[31] M. Agulhon, *The Republican Experiment, 1848–1852* (1983). Excellent general survey.

[32] P. Amman, *Revolution and Mass Democracy. The Paris Club Movement in 1848 France* (1975). Thoroughly researched.

[33] P. Bastid, *Doctrines et institutions politiques de la seconde république*, 2 vols (Paris, 1945). The best study of political ideas and institutions.

[34] E. Berenson, *Populist Religion and Left-Wing Politics in France, 1830–52* (1984). A study of political propaganda and its impact.

[35] R. Bezucha, 'Masks of Revolution: A Study of Popular Culture during the Second French Republic', in R. Price (ed.), *Revolution and Reaction. 1848 and the Second French Republic* (1975). The politicisation of traditional culture.

[36] J. P. T. Bury and R. P. Tombs, *Thiers, 1979–1877. A Political Life* (1986). A major study of a key political figure.

[37] P. Chalmin *et al.*, *L'Armée et la seconde république* (Paris, 1955).

[38] J. Dagnan, *Le Gers sous la seconde république*, 2 vols, (Auch, 1928). Brings local politics to life.

[39] T. R. Forstenzer, *French Provincial Police and the Fall of the Second Republic. Social Fear and Counter-Revolution* (1981). Informative, but greatly exaggerates the novelty of his thesis.

[40] W. Fortescue, *Alphonse de Lamartine. A Political Biography* (1983). Reliable study of the leading politician of early 1848.

[41] R. Gossez, 'Diversité des antagonismes sociaux vers le milieu du XIXe

siècle', *Revue économique* 7 (1956). A valuable warning against simplistic sociological analysis.

[42] R. Gossez, *Les Ouvriers de Paris* (Paris, 1967). Not an easy read, but rewarding.

[43] J. M. House, 'Civil-Military Relations in Paris, 1848', in R. Price (ed.), *Revolution and Reaction. 1848 and the Second French Republic* (1975).

[44] L. C. Jennings, *France and Europe in 1848* (1973). Especially good on policy towards Italy.

[45] C. H. Johnson, 'Economic Change and Artisan Discontent: The Tailor's History, 1800–1848', in R. Price (ed.), *Revolution and Reaction. 1848 and the Second French Republic* (1975). An insight into the politicisation of key professional groups.

[46] R. L. Koepke, 'The Failure of Parliamentary Government in France, 1840–48', *European Studies Review*, 9 (1979).

[47] E. Labrousse (ed.), *Aspects de la crise et de la dépression de l'économie française au milieu du XIXe siècle, 1846–52* (Paris, 1956). Studies of the economic crisis in a number of regions.

[48] R. Liebman, 'Repressive Stategies and Working-Class Protest: Lyon 1848–1852', *Social Science History*, 11 (1980).

[49] F. A. de Luna, *The French Republic under Cavaignac, 1848* (1969). A major study of the republic general who crushed the June insurrection.

[50] H. Machin, 'The Prefects and Political Repression: February 1848 to December 1851', in R. Price (ed.), *Revolution and Reaction. 1848 and the Second French Republic* (1975).

[51] R. W. Magraw, 'Pierre Joigneaux and Socialist Propaganda in the French Countryside', *French Historical Studies*, 10 (1977–78).

[52] T. Margadant, *French Peasants in Revolt. The Insurrection of 1851* (1979). Invaluable, although the application of modernisation theory is not always convincing.

[53] P. McPhee, 'The Seed-Time of the Republic: Society and Politics in the Pyrénées-Orientales, 1848–51', *Politics and History* (1976).

[54] J. M. Merriman, *The Agony of the Republic. The Repression of the Left in Revolutionary France, 1848–51* (1978). Excellent survey of the various forms of repression.

[55] R. Price, *The French Second Republic: A Social History* (1972). Not for me to comment! See R. Gildea, 'scholarly and reliable' in *Barricades and Borders. Europe, 1800–1914* (Oxford, 1987).

[56] R. Price (ed.), *Revolution and Reaction. 1848 and the Second French Republic* (1975). Contains a range of useful essays.

[57] R. Price (ed.), *1848 in France* (1975). A collection of documents with an introduction.

[58] R. Price, 'Techniques of Repression: the Control of Popular Protest in mid-Nineteenth Century France', *Historical Journal*, 25 (1982).

[59] R. Price, 'Poor Relief and Social Crisis in mid-Nineteenth-Century France', *European History Quarterly*, 13 (1983).

[60] R. Price, 'Subsistence Crises and Popular Protest', in *The Modernisation of Rural France* (1983). Examines the last major subsistence crises, and explains their disappearance.

[61] W. H. Sewell Jr., *Work and Revolution in France. The Language of Labor from the Old Regime to 1848* (1980). Stresses the continuities in work organisation and attitudes.

[62] M. L. Stewart-McDougall, *The Artisan Republic. Revolution, Reaction and Resistance in Lyon, 1848–51* (Gloucester, 1984). Important study of a city with an old radical tradition.

[63] C. Tilly, 'The People of June' in R. Price (ed.), *Revolution and Reaction. 1848 and the Second French Republic.* (1975).

[64] A. de Tocqueville, *Recollections* (1986). The views of an intelligent contemporary observer.

[65] M. Traugott, *Armies of the Poor. Determinants of Working Class Participation in the Parisian Insurrection of June, 1848* (1985). Considers why workers fought on both sides during the insurrection.

[66] A.-J. Tudesq, *Les Grands notables en France (1840–1849): études historique d'une psychologie sociale*, 2 vols (Paris, 1964). A massive study of social elites.

[67] A.-J. Tudesq, *L'Election présidentielle de Louis-Napoléon Bonaparte, 10 décembre, 1848* (Paris, 1965). Superb electoral study.

[68] P. Vigier, *La Seconde république dans la région alpine*, 2 vols (Paris, 1963).

[69] P. Vigier, *La Seconde république* (Paris, 1967).

[70] P. Vigier, 'Le Bonapartisme et le monde rurale', in K. Hammer and P. C. Hartmann (eds), *Der Bonapartismus. Historisches Phänomen und politischer Mythos* (Munich, 1977).

[71] P. Vigier, *La Vie quotidienne en province et à Paris pendant les journées de 1848* (Paris, 1982). A series of local *vignettes*.

[72] E. Weber, 'The Second Republic, Politics and the Peasant', *French Historical Studies*, XI (1980).

[73] E. Weber, '"Comment la politique vint aux paysans": A Second Look at Peasant Politicization', *American Historical Review*, 87 (1982).

[74] V. Wright, 'The Coup d'état of December 1851: Repression and the Limits to Repression', in R. Price (ed.), *Revolution and Reaction. 1848 and the Second French Republic* (1975).

Germany

[75] J. Bergmann, 'Ökonomische Voraussetzungen der Revolution von 1848. Zur Krise von 1845 bis 1848 in Deutschland' in H. U. Wehler (ed.), *200 Jahre amerikanische Revolution und moderne Revolutionsforschung, Geschichte und Gesellschaft* (1976). Very useful survey of the pre-revolutionary crisis.

[76] J. Bergmann, 'Soziallage, Selbstveritändnis und Aktionsformen der Arbeiter in der Revolution von 1848', in H. Volkmann and J. Bergmann (eds), *Sozialer Protest* (Opladen, 1984).

[77] J. Bergmann, 'Die Revolution von 1848 als Modernisierunskrise. Zur Vorgeschichte der Revolution aus modernisierungs-theoretischer Sicht', in J. Bergmann *et al.*, *Arbeit, Mobilität, Partizipation, Protest* (Opladen, 1986).

[78] H. Best, *Wirtschaftskrise und Revolution. Handwerker und Arbeiter 1848/1849*

(Stuttgart, 1986). Importance of period for emerging working class.

[79] H. Best, *Interessenpolitik und nationale Integration 1848/49* (Göttingen, 1980). Effective analysis of competing interest groups.

[80] H. Best, 'Analysis of Content and Context of Historical Documents – The Case of Petitions to the Frankfurt National Assembly, 1848/49', in J. M. Clubb and F. L. Schauch (eds), *Quantitative-Sozialwissenscheftliche forschungen* (Stuttgart, 1980).

[81] D. Blackbourn and G. Eley, *The Peculiarities of German History. Bourgeois Society and Politics in Nineteenth Century Germany* (1985). Controversial contribution to a major debate.

[82] D. Blasius, *Bürgerliche Gesellschaft und Kriminalität. Zur Socialgeschichte Preussens im Vormärz* (Göttingen, 1978). Useful for background to revolution.

[83] H. Bleiber, 'Bauern und Landarbeit in der bürgerlich-demokratischen Revolution von 1848/49 in Deutschland', *Zeitschrift für Geschichtswissenschaft*, 17 (1969). Good survey of rural unrest.

[83a] W. Boldt, *Die Anfänge der deutscher Parteiwesens: Factionen, politische Vereine und Parteien in der Revolution 1848* (Paderborn, 1971). The formation of parties as seen by the press.

[84] W. Boldt, 'Konstitutionelle Monarchie oder parlamentarische Demokratie', *Historische Zeitschrift*, 216 (1973).

[85] M. Botzenhart, *Deutscher Parlamentarismus der Revolution zeit 1848–50* (Düsseldorf, 1977). Political and constitutional history.

[86] J. Calliess, *Militäs in der Krise. Die bayerische Armee in der Revolution 1848/49* (Boppard am Rhein, 1976). Insights into the key question of the role of the military.

[87] R. Canevdi, 'The "False French Alarm": Revolutionary Panic in Baden, 1848', *Central European History*, 18, (1985).

[88] D. Dowe, *Aktion und Organisation. Arbeiterbewegung, sozialistische und kommunistische Bewegung in der preussischen Rheinprovinz, 1820–1852* (Hannover, 1970). Important study of major centre of radicalism.

[89] J. Droz, *Les Révolutions allemandes de 1848* (Paris, 1957). Massive general study which takes account of regional variations. Insufficient analysis.

[90] F. Eyck, *The Frankfurt Parliament, 1848–49* (1968). Solid, reliable study.

[91] H. Fischer, 'Konservatismus von unten Wahlen im ländlichen Preussen 1849/52 – Organisation, Agitation, Manipulation', in D. Stegmann, B.-J. Wendt and P.-C. Wilt (eds), *Deutscher Konservatismus im 19 und 20 Jahrhundert* (Bonn, 1983). Good introduction to the development of political reaction.

[92] M. Gailus, 'Soziale Protest bewungen in Deutschland 1847–1849' in Volkmann and Bergmann (eds), *Sozialer Protest* (1984). Continuity and change in the forms of popular protest.

[93] J. R. Gillis, *The Prussian Bureaucracy in Crisis, 1840–1860* (1972). A means of understanding both the weaknesses and fundamental strength of the Prussian state.

[94] D. Groh, 'Le "Sonderweg". De l'histoire allemande: mythe ou réalité', *Annales ESC*, 38 (1983).

[95] D. Grünthal, *Parlamentarismus in Preussen 1848/49–1857/58* (Düsseldorf,

1982). A substantial constitutional and parliamentary history – considers the workings of the three-class system.

[96] E. Hahn, 'German Parliamentary National Aims in 1848–49: A Legacy Reassessed', *Central European History*, 13 (1980).

[97] F. S. Hamerow, 'History and the German Revolution of 1848', *American Historical Review*, 60 (1954).

[98] F. S. Hamerow, *Restoration, Revolution, Reaction* (1958). Still an useful introduction to the period.

[99] F. S. Hamerow, '1848', in L. Krieger and F. Stern, *The Responsibility of Power* (1968).

[100] R. Hoppe and J. Kuczynski, 'Eine Berufs-bzw. auch Klasses – und Schichtenanalyse der Märzgefallenen 1848 in Berlin', in *Jahrbuch für Wirtschaftsgeschichte*, IV (1964).

[101] H.-G. Husung, *Protest und Repression im Vormärz. Norddeutschland zwischen Restauration und Revolution* (Göttingen, 1983). Setting the revolution within its historical context.

[102] R. Koch, 'Die Agrarrevolution in Deutschland 1848', in D. Langewiesche (ed.), *Die deutsche Revolution von 1848/49* (Darmstadt, 1983).

[103] D. Langewiesche, 'Gesellschafts – und verfassungspolitische Handlungsbedingungen und Ziel vorstellungen europäscher Liberaler in der Revolutionen von 1848', in W. Schieder (ed.), *Liberalismus in der Gesellschaft des deutschen Vormärz* (Göttingen, 1983).

[104] D. Langewiesche, *Liberalismus und Demokratie in Würtemberg zwischen Revolution und Reichsgründung* (Düsseldorf, 1974). An important regional study.

[105] D. Langewiesche, 'Die Anfänge der deutschen Parteien. Partei, Fraktion und Verein in der Revolution von 1848/49', *Geschichte und Gesellschaft*, 4 (1978).

[106] D. Langewiesche, 'Republik, Konstitutionelle Monarchie und "Soziale Frage". Grundprobleme det deutschen Revolution von 1848/49', *Historische Zeitschrift*, 230 (1980).

[107] D. Langewiesche, 'Die deutsche Revolution von 1848/49 und die vorrevolutionäre Gesellschaft: Forschungsstand und Forschungsperspektives', *Archiv für Sozialgeschichte*, 21 (1981).

[108] D. Langewiesche (ed.) *Die deutsche Revolution von 1848/49* (Darmstadt, 1983). Good collection of articles on most aspects of the revolutionary period.

[109] A. Lüdtke, 'The Role of State Violence in the Period of Transition to Industrial Capitalism: the Example of Prussia from 1815 to 1848', *Social History*, 3 (1979).

[110] D. J. Mattheisen, 'History as Current Events: Recent Works on the German Revolution of 1848', *American Historical Review*, 88 (1983).

[111] J. Mooser, *Ländliche Klassengesellschaft*, 1770–1848 (Göttingen, 1985). A major study of the Westphalian peasantry.

[112] P. H. Noyes, *Organisation and Revolution. Working Class Associations in the German Revolution of 1848/49* (1966). A major study, well worth persevering with.

[113] L. O'Boyle, 'The Democratic Left in Germany, 1848', *Journal of Modern History*, XXXIII (1961).

[114] W. J. Orr, 'East Prussia and the Revolutions of 1848', *Central European History*, 13 (1980).

[114a] K. L. von Prittwitz, *Berlin 1848. Das Erinnerungswerk des Generalleutnants Karl Ludwig von Prittwitz und anderere Quellan zur Berliner Märzrevolution und zur Geschichte Preussens um die Mitte des 19. Jahrhunderts* (Berlin, 1985). New insights into military failure.

[115] W. Real, *Die Revolution in Baden, 1848/1849* (Stuttgart, 1983). Good study of a major centre of radical agitation.

[116] H. Rohlling, 'Das Sozialprofil der Hanover Turnerwehr 1849', in Volkmann and Bergmann (eds), *Sozialer Protest* (Opladen, 1984).

[117] H.-J. Rupieper, 'Die Sozialstruktur der Trägerschichten der Revolution 1848/49 am Beispiel Sachsen', in H. Kaelble *et al.* (eds), *Probleme der Modernisierung in Deutschland* (Opladen, 1978).

[118] W. Schieder, 'Die Rolle der deutschen Arbeiter in der Revolution von 1848/49', in W. Klötzer *et al.*, *Ideen und Strukturen der deutschen Revolution 1848* (Frankfurt a M, 1974).

[119] J. Sheehan, *German Liberalism in the Nineteenth Century* (1978). Major study setting 1848 liberalism within its historical context.

[120] E. Shorter, 'Middle Class Anxiety in the German Revolution of 1848', *Journal of Social History*, 2 (1968–9).

[121] W. Siemann, *Die Frankfurter Nationalversammlung. Die Bedeutung der Juristendominanz* (Berne, 1976).

[122] W. Siemann, *Restauration, Liberalismus und nationale Bewegung (1815–1870)* (Darmstadt, 1982).

[123] W. Siemann, *Die deutsche Revolution von 1848–49* (Frankfurt, 1985). Useful synthesis.

[124] R. Stadelmann, *Social and Political History of the German 1848 Revolution* (Athens, Ohio, 1978).

[125] R. Tilly, 'Popular Disorders in Nineteenth Century Germany', *Journal of Social History*, 4 (1970–1).

[126] V. Valentin, *Geschichte der deutschen Revolution von 1848–1849* 2, vols (Berlin, 1931). Old but still useful, as is the one-volume English edition.

[127] H. Volkmann and J. Bergmann (eds), *Sozialer Protest. Studien zu traditioneller Resistenz und Kollektiver Gewalt in Deutschland vom Vormärz bis zur Reichsgründung* (Opladen, 1984).

[128] M. Walker, *German Home Towns. Community, State, General Estates* (Ithaca, N.Y., 1971). Useful for setting the context for political activity.

[129] R. Weber, *Die Beziehungen zwischen sozialer Struktur und politischer Ideologie des Kleinbürgertums in der Revolution von 1848/49* (1965). Offers insights into the complexities of socio-political analysis.

[130] R. Wirtz, 'Die Begriffsverwirrung der Bauern im Odenwald 1848', in D. Puls (ed.), *Wahrnehmungsformen und Protestverhalted* (Frankfurt a M, 1979).

[131] G. Wollstein, *Das 'Gross deutschland' der Paulskirche: Nationale Ziele in*

107

der *bürgerlichen Revolution 1848–1849* (Düsseldorf, 1977). Together with the next title, this provides an important study of nationalism.

[132] G. Wollstein, *Mitteleuropa und Grossdeutschland – Visionen der Revolution 1848/49. Nationale Ziele in der deutschen Revolution* (1980).

The Habsburg Empire

[133] R. A. Austensen, 'The Making of Austria's Prussian Policy, 1848–52', *Historical Journal*, xxvii (1984).

[134] I. Deak, 'Destruction, Revolution, or Reform: Hungary on the Eve of 1848', *Austrian History Yearbook* xii–xiii (1976–7).

[135] I. Deak, *The Lawful Revolution: Louis Kossuth and the Hungarians, 1848–49* (1979). Comprehensive survey of events.

[136] I. Deak, 'An Army Divided: The Loyalty Crisis of the Habsburg Officer Corps in 1848–1849', *Jahrbuch des Instituts für Deutsche Geschichte*, 8 (1979).

[137] R. R. Florescu, 'Debunking a Myth: The Magyar–Romanian Struggle of 1848–1849', *Austrian History Yearbook* xii–xiii (1976–7).

[138] G. Handlery, 'Revolutionary Organisation in the Context of Backwardness: Hungary's 1848', *East European Quarterly*, 6 (1972).

[139] B. H. Király (ed.), *East Central European Society and War in the Era of Revolutions, 1775–1856* (New York, 1984). An important collection of articles.

[140] A. Klíma, 'The Bourgeois Revolution of 1848–1849 in Central Europe', in R. Porter and M. Teich, *Revolution in History* (1986).

[141] S. Z. Pech, *The Czech Revolution of 1848* (Chapel Hill, N.C., 1969). Sound and informative.

[142] J. Polisensky, *Aristocrats and the Crown in the Revolutionary Year 1848* (Albany, N.Y., 1980). Marxist view of the Czech revolution.

[143] R. J. Rath, *The Viennese Revolution of 1848* (Austin, Texas, 1957). Thorough – wears his conservative political views on his sleeve.

[144] R. L. Rudolph, 'Economic Revolution in Austria? The Meaning of 1848 in Austrian Economic History', in J. Komlos (ed.), *Economic Development in the Habsberg Monarchy in the Nineteenth Century*. (1985).

[145] A. Sked, *The Survival of the Habsburg Empire: Radetzky, the Imperial Army and the Class War, 1848* (1979). Excellent on the role of the army in Lombardy–Venetia.

[146] István Széchenyi, 'Miklós Wesselényi, Lajos Kossuth and the Problem of Romanian Nationalism', *Austrian History Yearbook* xii–xiii (1976–7).

[147] J. F. Zacek, 'Czech Attitudes towards the Hungarian Revolution', *Austrian History Yearbook* xii–xiii (1976–7).

Italy

[147a] D. Demarco, 'Le rivoluzioni italiano de 1848', in *Studi in onore di Gino Luzzatto* (Milan, 1950).

[148] A. M. Ghisalberti, *Momenti e figure del Risorgimento romano* (Milan, 1965).
[149] P. Ginsborg, 'Peasants and Revolutionaries in Venice and Veneto, 1848', *Historical Journal*, 17 (1974).
[150] P. Ginsborg, *Daniel Manin and the Venetian Revolution of 1848–1849* (1979). Very good in depth study.
[151] B. F. Griffith, 'Italian Nationalism and Particularities in 1848: The Example of Tuscany', in H. T. Parker (ed.), *The Consortium in Revolutionary Europe. Proceedings.* (1975).
[152] H. Hearder, 'The Making of the Roman Republic, 1848–1849', *History*, LX (1975).
[153] H. Hearder, *Italy in the Age of the Risorgimento* (1983). Informative, perhaps a little lacking in analysis.
[154] F. della Peruta, *Democrazia e socialismo nel risorgimento* (Rome, 1977).
[155] C. Ronchi, *I democratici Fiorentini nella rivoluzione del' 1848–49* (Florence, 1963).
[156] S. Woolf, *A History of Italy, 1700–1860: the Social Constraints of Political Change* (1979). Sets the historical context.

United Kingdom

[157] H. M. Boot, *The Commercial Crisis of 1847* (Hull, 1984). Shows why the economic crisis was less severe in Britain than elsewhere.
[158] J. Epstein and D. Thompson (eds), *The Chartist Experience. Studies in Working-Class Radicalism and Culture* (1982). Excellent collection of articles.
[159] D. Goodway, *London Chartism, 1838–1848* (1982). Central to an understanding of events in the capital.
[160] F. C. Mather, *Public Order in the Age of the Chartists* (Manchester, 1959). Useful study of the problems faced by the authorities.
[161] G. Rudé, 'Why was there no Revolution in England in 1830 or 1848?' in M. Kossok (ed.), *Studien über die Revolution* (Berlin, 1971).
[162] J. Saville, *1848. The British State and the Chartist Movement* (1987). A major reassessment of the Chartist threat and of government policy.
[163] M. I. Thomas and P. Holt, *Threats of Revolution in Britain, 1789–1848* (1977). Assesses the seriousness of the menace of revolution.
[164] D. Thompson, *The Chartists* (1984). Good synthesis of recent work.
[165] H. Weisser, 'Chartism in 1848: Reflections on a non-Revolution', *Albion*, 13 (1981).

Others

[166] D. R. Headrick, 'Spain and the Revolutions of 1848', *European Studies Review*, 6 (1976).

Index

111

112

113

115

116